BROTHERS AT WAR

Israel and the Tragedy of the *Altalena*

Jerold S. Auerbach

Quid Pro Books

New Orleans, Louisiana

Copyright © 2011 by Jerold S. Auerbach. All rights reserved. This book or parts of it may not be reproduced, copied, or transmitted (except as permitted by sections 107 and 108 of the U.S. Copyright Law and except by reviewers for the public press), by any means including voice recordings and the copying of its digital form, without the written permission of the publisher.

Published by Quid Pro Books.

ISBN: 1-61027-061-4 (pbk)

Quid Pro, LLC
5860 Citrus Blvd., Suite D-101
New Orleans, Louisiana 70123
www.quidprobooks.com

For bulk orders, school adoptions, review copies, and information on available ebook formats and classroom uses, please contact the publisher at info@quidprobooks.com.

Cover photograph taken by Robert Capa in 1948, presently under copyright with Magnum Photos, New York. Reproduced under license by Magnum Photos. Title page photograph by Hans Pinn. Reprinted with permission of the National Photo Collection, State of Israel.

Publisher's Cataloging-in-Publication

Auerbach, Jerold S.
    Brothers at war: Israel and the tragedy of the *Altalena* / Jerold S. Auerbach.
        p. cm.
    Includes index and bibliographical references.

ISBN: 1610270606 (hc)
ISBN-13: 9781610270601 (hc)
ISBN: 1610270614 (pbk)
ISBN-13: 9781610270618 (pbk)
ISBN-13: 9781610270625 (Kindle)
ISBN-13: 9781610270632 (ePub)

"A probing and poignant exploration of the tragedy of the *Altalena*, the doomed ship whose arrival in Israel in 1948 ignited Jewish fratricidal conflict only weeks after the declaration of statehood."

1. Israel—History—1948. 2. Jewish-Arab Relations—1948-1967. 3. Israel—Politics and government—20th century. I. Title. II. Auerbach, Jerold S.

DS128.4.A16 2011   946.9433'2—dc20

For Haggai

My Friend, My Teacher

"The past is never dead.
It's not even past."

Requiem for a Nun
William Faulkner

Contents

Introduction..1

1. Groundless Hatred..7
2. Conflict in Zion..19
3. Civil War?..41
4. Competing Truths...89
5. Memories..117

Epilogue..135

    Bibliographical Note...143

    Acknowledgments..153

    About the Author..155

    Index..157

Brothers at War

Introduction

Barely a month after the birth of the State of Israel on May 14, 1948, the fledgling nation approached the brink of civil war. Amid its desperate struggle for survival against invading armies from five Arab countries, the arrival of a ship named *Altalena* provoked a violent and traumatic confrontation. For some embattled participants it even evoked memories of Jerusalem in the 1st century, when a Jewish civil war shredded national sovereignty for nearly two thousand years. The dark shadow of the *Altalena* still hovers over Israel more than six decades later, raising vital issues of political legitimacy that have yet to be resolved in the Jewish state.

The *Altalena* story braids themes that are woven into ancient Jewish sources and modern Jewish experiences. The book of Genesis recounts that in the beginning, after Creation went awry, Noah's ark — the first ship to be mentioned in a Jewish text — transported a righteous man and his family from impending disaster to safety. Jews sailed to safe haven in America as early as 1654, when twenty-three refugees from Brazil landed in New Amsterdam. In the mid-19th century, as many as 200,000 German Jewish immigrants arrived in the United States. Then, during the decades surrounding the turn of the twentieth century, nearly two million Jews fled from poverty and persecution in Eastern Europe. Packed on board teeming immigrant ships, those uprooted Jews were among the "huddled masses yearning to breathe free" — in the memorable words of Emma Lazarus that were engraved beneath the Statue of Liberty. Their flight from danger, combined with their yearning for freedom in a safe homeland, is deeply embedded in American Jewish history.

With Adolf Hitler's ascent to power in Germany in 1933, and the inexorable spread of Nazi terror throughout Europe, frantic Jews tried to flee from imminent danger and looming annihilation. They rarely succeeded. Restrictive American immigration laws, government indifference to the plight of European Jewry, and the fearful timidity of American Jews kept them away. For all but a fortunate few, the possibility of reaching the *goldene medina*, their American Zion, vanished. By the end of the Thirties, British restrictions on Jewish immigration had also placed Palestine, where Zionists were building a new society in the biblical homeland of the Jewish people, beyond reach.

Jewish desperation reached its tragic climax on "voyages of the damned." In May 1939 the *St. Louis* departed from Hamburg with 937 German Jews on board. Denied permission by the government of Cuba to disembark its passengers it sailed away, passing within view of Miami. But neither President Roosevelt nor the State Department would stretch immigration quotas to save Jewish lives. The *St. Louis* returned to Germany, where many of its passengers perished in the Holocaust. Then, in November 1940, Jewish refugees on board the *Patria* awaited deportation from Haifa after British authorities shut the gates of entry into Palestine. An unexpectedly powerful bomb, smuggled on board by a Haganah agent to prevent its departure, sank the ship within fifteen minutes, killing 260 passengers.

One year later, in December 1941, a decrepit Greek vessel, the *Struma*, left Romania for Palestine. On board were 769 Jewish refugees, including 103 children. After three days at sea, engine failure forced it to be towed into Istanbul harbor, where it was placed under quarantine. Turkish authorities would not permit the passengers to disembark and the British government, as its ambassador bluntly stated, "did not want these people in Palestine." After two months of futile negotiations, while the refugees languished on board without adequate food or medical care, the Turkish government ordered the hapless ship towed back into the Black Sea. One day later, struck by a torpedo from a Soviet submarine, the *Struma* exploded and sank. Nineteen year-old David Stolier was the sole survivor.

After the Holocaust barely a surviving Jewish remnant remained alive to seek refuge in Palestine. Once again, ships attempted to transport Jews to safety and freedom. But unrelenting Arab hostility to Jewish immigration was reinforced by British capitulation (fed by

INTRODUCTION

lurking anti-Semitism) to Arab demands. The yearning of Jews for Zion, where they could build a state of their own, was repeatedly and cruelly thwarted.

The inspirational journey of one ship, the *Exodus*, has testified ever since to the fierce determination of Holocaust survivors to reach "*Altneuland*," the old-new land of Theodor Herzl's dream. The story of the *Exodus* has been endlessly told, retold, celebrated — and popularized in the romantic novel by Leon Uris that was transformed into an iconic Hollywood movie. The poignant journey of its passengers in 1947 — from France to Palestine, then back to France and, finally, to displaced persons camps in Germany — came to symbolize the desperate yearning of the Jewish people. It remains embedded in the heroic narrative of the creation of the State of Israel — and the history of British perfidy.

One year later, barely a month after proclaiming its independence, the new Jewish state was besieged by invading Arab armies determined to destroy it. Amid its desperate struggle for survival the *Altalena*, a ship dispatched by the Irgun Zvai Leumi (National Military Organization), led by Menachem Begin, arrived in Israel with more than nine hundred fighters and desperately needed weapons and munitions. But Prime Minister David Ben-Gurion, perceiving a menacing challenge to the state and to his authority, seized the opportunity to quash his detested right-wing political rivals. Claiming that the *Altalena* was the spearhead of a *putsch*, an attempt to overthrow the government, he ordered the Israel Defense Forces to destroy it.

The story of the *Altalena*, with its bloody climax, reveals another enduring theme in Jewish history, the recurrent tragedy of sibling rivalry and fratricide. That, too, is grounded in the biblical narrative. Cain murdered Abel. Isaac robbed Ishmael of his inheritance. Jacob's deception gained him Esau's birthright. Joseph's brothers, tormented by jealousy, abandoned him to die in a deep pit. In 1st century Jerusalem, Jewish Zealots ruthlessly slaughtered their fellow Jews in a civil war that destroyed the Temple, the revered religious and symbolic center of Jewish life and, with it, national sovereignty.

Finally restored to their homeland after nineteen centuries of exile, Jews once again turned violently against their brothers. In June 1948 Israeli soldiers opened fire against Jewish fighters from the *Altalena* who had arrived to join in the struggle for independence. After a two-day battle, the ship was shelled and destroyed. Few Israelis now remember the *Altalena*, and hardly anyone outside Israel has even heard of it. But the *Altalena* tragedy remains a sorrowful reminder that baseless hatred — known ever since the destruction of the Second Temple in 70 CE as *sinat hinam* — continued to torment the Jewish people, even at their wondrous moment of national rebirth.

Israelis on the political left still claim that Menachem Begin's Irgun received what it deserved for daring to challenge the legitimacy of the government of the new Jewish state and the authority of its prime minister. For those on the political right, however, Ben-Gurion acted with ruthless determination to delegitimize, even destroy, his political opposition, causing the deaths of 16 Irgun fighters and 3 Israeli soldiers. Whether such conflicting memories of that tragic episode will deter the recurrence of internecine Jewish violence — or encourage it — remains an open question.

Although the *Exodus* and the *Altalena* are forever embedded in the remarkable story of the birth of Israel, they endure as contradictory symbols of the struggle for Jewish statehood. The *Exodus*, admired as the valiant ship, epitomized the desperate yearning of Holocaust survivors to reach their historic homeland. The *Altalena*, castigated as the pariah ship, ignited a bitter struggle of "brother against brother" whose reverberations can still be felt in the Jewish state.

The story of that pariah ship remains to be told. This is the first history of the *Altalena* to be published in more than thirty years, the first in English, and the first to be written by a historian. But it is not merely the chronicle of a doomed ship — however compelling, disturbing, and instructive that might be. It locates the *Altalena*, and

INTRODUCTION

the fierce battle triggered by its arrival in Israel, within the historical framework of Jewish fratricidal conflict. Then it explores the internal Zionist struggle in Palestine that was the prelude — at times vicious and violent — to the bloody confrontation in June 1948.

Brothers at War sharply challenges the conventional wisdom regarding David Ben-Gurion's leadership during the *Altalena* crisis. Celebrating his extraordinary achievement as the founding father of the first sovereign Jewish state in two thousand years, his defenders have claimed that he justifiably used military force to save the fragile new nation. The very survival of Israel, they insist, turned on Ben-Gurion's order to open fire.

This book rejects those conclusions, and their implicit corollary that at a critical moment in Israel's struggle for independence Menachem Begin recklessly brought the new nation to the brink of civil war. Yearning to participate in that struggle and contribute to it, Begin was targeted by Ben-Gurion's wrath — and guns. But while Ben-Gurion ordered Israeli soldiers to shoot fellow Jews, Begin commanded his loyal fighters not to return fire. His insistence upon restraint demonstrated his unyielding determination to prevent civil war from once again dividing the Jewish people and shattering Jewish sovereignty, as it had done nineteen centuries earlier.

For many years the *Altalena* sank beneath Israeli consciousness. But just as memories of the civil war in ancient Jerusalem hovered over the *Altalena* in 1948, so a phantom "*Altalena*," the memory of that modern tragedy, continues to resurface. During the past decade *Altalena* analogies have punctuated Israeli political debate. Now the *Altalena* is linked to the volatile issue of Jewish settlements in Judea and Samaria, the biblical homeland of the Jewish people. If tens of thousands of religious settlers should refuse to leave their homes under an Israeli-Palestinian peace accord, would the government of Israel respond with guns and bullets as it did in 1948? What if religious soldiers did not obey orders to forcibly expel them? Israelis may once again confront their nagging "*Altalena*" question: When, if ever, is it right to disobey orders that may be wrong?

BROTHERS AT WAR

At stake in this simmering conflict, as it was during the *Altalena* confrontation, is the vexing problem of political legitimacy. To be sure, as German sociologist Max Weber wrote, a state must claim a monopoly on "the legitimate use of physical force." But a crucial component of legitimacy, historian Bernard Lewis suggests, is the presence of a political leader who "does not need to use excessive force or brutality to maintain himself in power." The story of the *Altalena* illuminates this enduring conundrum, while revealing the flaws and strengths of David Ben-Gurion and Menachem Begin as political leaders.

Haunting questions from the outburst of fratricidal violence that erupted with the arrival of the *Altalena* still hover over Israel. Must soldiers always obey orders? Whose commands must they obey: those of their officers or those of their conscience? When may they disobey? No less vital, when can the government of the Jewish state resort to violence against its citizens without compromising its own legitimacy? Amid the unremitting assaults on Israel's legitimacy that swirl throughout the Muslim Middle East, which already corrupt political and academic discourse in the West, these are hardly frivolous questions. The answers, and the lessons that continue to be drawn from the war between brothers in 1948, may determine the future of Israel.

Chapter 1
Groundless Hatred

The Jews of Jotapata, a fortress city in the northern Galilee, had endured brutal siege warfare from Roman soldiers for forty-seven days. Then, under cover of darkness, a handful of warriors from the Fifteenth Legion cut the throats of the night watchmen and entered the city gates. Soldiers swarmed after them, sparing few lives as they relentlessly pursued Jews in their homes and hiding places. It was recorded that forty thousand Jewish men were slain. Anticipating their inevitable fate, Jewish soldiers committed suicide in droves. "And thus was Jotapata taken, in the thirteenth year of the reign of Nero," on the first day of the Hebrew month of Tammuz in 67 CE.

The commander of the Jewish army in Jotapata, who subsequently authored the chronicle of its destruction, was Yosef ben Matityahu ha-Kohen. Named in honor of his distinguished Hasmonean ancestors (remembered in history as the Maccabees), he is better known as Flavius Josephus, the famous — some would say infamous — author of *The Wars of the Jews; or, The History of the Destruction of Jerusalem*. His dramatic, indeed flamboyant, narrative of that devastating conflict and its consequences remains the unrivaled description of the catastrophic destruction of Jewish national sovereignty. In *Wars of the Jews*, Josephus — priestly aristocrat, military commander (and deserter), chronicler (and myth-maker) — recounted the civil war that would form a backdrop to the trauma of the *Altalena* nearly nineteen hundred years later.

Josephus had been born into a family of wealth and influence within the Jewish ruling elite in Jerusalem. A visit to Rome, probably in 63 CE — three years before the Jewish revolt erupted — introduced him to his privileged Roman counterparts, who may have influenced his perception of the gathering conflict in his Judaean homeland. Upon his return to Jerusalem he warned his people, who seemed "wildly enthusiastic" about rebellion, "not to be so reckless, not so crazy as to expose their land and families and themselves to the most dreadful danger." But they did not heed his admonitions. With the outbreak of war Josephus — as befitting a member of the ruling class — was assigned military command in the Galilee. He served there until the siege of Jotapata propelled him into his new career as the chronicler of national catastrophe and his own survival.

With Jotapata under assault, and the defeat of his battalions and his own likely death imminent, Josephus abandoned his soldiers and took refuge in a cave among "forty persons of eminence." On his third day in hiding, their location was revealed to Vespasian, the Roman commander, who demanded their surrender. Josephus, as was customary for the member of a priestly family from Jerusalem, prayed for divine guidance. He reassured God: "I do not go over to the Romans as a deserter of the Jews, but as a minister from thee." But if Josephus was persuaded of his own divine inspiration and rectitude, his underground companions were understandably enraged. How could a self-proclaimed leader of the Jews, who had urged them "to lose their lives for liberty," contemplate betrayal and surrender?

The furious defectors offered Josephus their "right hand and a sword" with the stark choice: to die as a Jewish general or as a traitor. It was, Josephus conceded, "a brave thing to die for liberty." So he proposed that they all die together, in a sequence to be determined by drawing lots. Whether "by chance" or "by the providence of God" (as Josephus wrote) — but more likely by his mendacious manipulation — Josephus and another Jew managed to save their own lives and offered to surrender. Led to Vespasian, and claiming to be a divine messenger, Josephus hailed the newest conqueror of the Jews as "Caesar and emperor." Rewarded for his flattering prophecy with "suits of clothes, and other precious gifts," Josephus was spared for his future as the Roman patrician who would chronicle the doomed rebellion of his people, whose soldiers he had abandoned to save his own life.

Josephus's *Wars of the Jews* still frames our understanding of the national tragedy that has resonated in Jewish history ever since. It is a fascinating, compelling, puzzling, and unabashedly self-serving story. Eyewitness and participant in the events he recounted, Josephus documented in gruesome detail the horrific warfare that destroyed the Jewish nation. Historians continue to debate the veracity of his narrative, but his chilling rendition of the civil war between Jews that undermined their state from within, while Roman legions besieged Jerusalem from its ramparts, remains deeply embedded in Jewish memory.

It was, Josephus lamented, the "seditious temper" of his people that destroyed "my own country." In that "bitter contest between those that were fond of war, and those that were desirous of peace," he blamed "tyrants among the Jews who brought the Roman power upon us, who unwillingly attacked us, and occasioned the burning of our holy temple." In this desperate struggle for survival between the "Zealots" (whom he despised) and the besieged "multitude," the Zealots had descended into "barbarity." As Josephus wrote: they "trampled upon all the laws of man, and laughed at the laws of God."

So Josephus, the Jewish general who deserted his soldiers and betrayed his companions in hiding by saving his life at their expense, became the Roman historian who acclaimed the conquerors of his people. But his "instinct for apologetic," as historian Martin Goodman suggests, "overcame his conscience as a historian." Josephus deftly shifted blame for defeat from the attacking Roman legions, to which he had sworn allegiance at Jotapata, to the Jews he had abandoned. Throughout his account, he pilloried "deceivers and imposters," "false prophets," "charlatans," "brigands," "rogue Jews," "revolutionaries," "Zealots" and "*sicarii*" (vicious knife-wielders) who were engaged in "seditious practices" against the peaceful Jewish citizens of Jerusalem — the elite to which Josephus belonged.

Recounting "the calamities and slaughter" that Jews inflicted upon each other, Josephus observed that even Vespasian was stunned by their ferocity. Cautioning his warriors not to plunge into battle against such fanatics, the Roman general and future emperor — precisely as Josephus had predicted — instructed them: "The Jews are vexed to pieces every day by their civil wars and dissensions, and are under greater misfortunes than, if they were once taken, could be inflicted on them by us." For their own safety, therefore, Roman soldiers must "permit those Jews to destroy one another."

Josephus's privileged position, shifting allegiances, and scathing judgments continue to provoke debate and disagreement. Was he a realist, a traitor, or a martyr — a Jewish nationalist or a Roman loyalist, as suited his convenience and preserved his life? He was, Goodman concludes, "inclined to believe the worst of all those Jews who had not, like him, recognized the divine will and accordingly stopped opposing Rome." His virulent hostility toward the Zealots — "nor was there any previous villainy recorded in history," Josephus wrote, "that they failed zealously to emulate" — served as an apology for his own behavior. The more he could blame Zealots for the national catastrophe, the easier it was to exonerate the Romans — and justify his own betrayal. By surrendering to Roman authorities Josephus managed to perform a "legendary act of abandonment and reclamation." His defection, Israeli sociologist Nachman Ben-Yehuda has concluded, forever marks him as "one of the worst traitors in Jewish history."

Josephus's stark and dramatic narrative, built as it was on the foundation of his pro-Roman and anti-Zealot bias, remains irresistibly compelling. In it, the prominent and respectable classes in Jerusalem who were desperate to prevent war — comprising the priesthood, "the powerful," and "notable" — confronted "the revolutionaries," "insurgents," and "Zealots" who were determined to provoke the conflagration that ultimately destroyed both the city and the nation. For Josephus, the choice between them — once his life was at stake — was easy.

In framing the narrative of the struggle — and the lessons that would be drawn from it, Josephus had virtually no competitors. His sharply binary story of good and evil in 1st century Jerusalem may be "full of polemic and apologetic," but its authority nonetheless endures. "There is only one account," historian James McLaren writes — "and it is one-sided." But Josephus's history of the Jewish wars has never been superseded, nor is it ever likely to be.

GROUNDLESS HATRED

Yet at the core of *Wars of the Jews* is a contradiction, wrapped within a paradox, with enduring implications for the modern State of Israel. Josephus detested the Zealots as "murderous fanatics" who were driven by religious frenzy. In Jerusalem they were "the dregs of society, the bastard scum . . . of our nation." Nonetheless — and, considering his palpable loathing for them, astonishingly — he famously lauded the Zealots as the heroes of Masada, the mountaintop fortress that became the site of the final tragedy of the Roman war. How, wonders historian Tessa Rajak, "are we to explain why Josephus highlighted and appeared to eulogise the fate of the last of the detested rebels whom he had up to that moment not ceased to denounce?"

This is an important question, not only for understanding the Masada story, which became deeply embedded in Zionist mythology and Israeli folklore. It has framed the lessons that Israelis have drawn from the Roman war about the political consequences of excessive, especially religious, zeal — now an ever more contentious and divisive issue in the Jewish state. The Masada story line, as narrated by Josephus, is familiar to Jews. In 73 CE, three years after Jerusalem had fallen and Jewish resistance elsewhere had collapsed under the awesome might of Roman military power, the most extreme Zealots — excoriated by Josephus as *sicarii* — gathered in their mountaintop fortress overlooking the Dead Sea for their last stand against the formidable Tenth Roman Legion.

After several months of siege, their leader Elazar ben Yair realized that the imminent Roman assault offered "no other way of escaping, or room for further courage." So, in his memorable final speech to his followers, he declared (as Josephus wrote):

> Since we long ago . . . resolved never to be servants to the Romans, nor to any other than to God himself, who alone is the true and just Lord of mankind, the time is now come that obliges us to make that resolution true in practice. . . . We were the very first that revolted from them and we are the last that fight against them; and I cannot but esteem it as a favor that God hath granted us, that it is still in our power to die bravely, and in a state of freedom.

BROTHERS AT WAR

The choice that Elazar ben Yair presented to his fighters was to kill their own family members before killing each other — or be slaughtered by Roman soldiers. "Miserable men indeed were they," Josephus writes, "whose distress forced them to slay their own wives and children with their own hands, as the lightest of those evils that were before them." With their grisly task accomplished, they cast lots to select ten men who would kill the others, until the last survivor fell on his sword. The next morning, when Roman warriors swarmed over Masada, they discovered the bodies of 960 Zealots. Denied the joy of victory, Josephus recounts, the Roman soldiers nonetheless admired the extraordinary courage of their enemies, zealous to their self-inflicted tragic end.

Josephus's account of Masada was narrated to him — he claimed — by two elderly women who had survived the slaughter hiding in a cistern. Solitary witnesses to the calamity, they described its horror. No confirming evidence exists from any other source. There are no remotely comparable episodes of collective Jewish suicide — actually murder, since only the last survivor killed himself — with one conspicuous exception. It is found in Josephus's own account of the battle of Jotapata six years earlier, when he had commanded — and then abandoned — Jewish soldiers while choosing surrender and life over bravery and death.

Strangely, the very Zealots whom Josephus castigated for their "wild and brutish disposition" and destructive fanaticism in Jerusalem were elevated into brave heroes for their death pact at Masada. Josephus praised no Jews more lavishly than those who chose murder (with a solitary suicide) as the ultimate heroic act, preferring to die by their own hands rather than fight to the death against Roman soldiers. (Perhaps Josephus admired them for doing what he had not done.) Incurring Josephus's condemnation when they fought against Roman warriors in Jerusalem, the Zealots became virtuous heroes when they slaughtered each other at Masada.

The enduring lesson of the loss of Jerusalem, followed by the Masada tragedy, was taught by ancient rabbis, the new leaders of the

GROUNDLESS HATRED

Jewish community after the final collapse of national sovereignty. Struggling to comprehend this calamity, they recognized that the Jews of Jerusalem had been renowned for their study of Torah, observance of the commandments, and generosity to the poor. These obligations, faithfully discharged, had been the traditional foundation pillars of Jewish personal and communal responsibility. Why, then, was the Temple destroyed? Because, the rabbis concluded sorrowfully, Jerusalem had been ravaged by "hatred without cause." Such "gratuitous" hatred, displayed by Jews toward other Jews, was the equivalent of "the three sins of idolatry, immorality, and bloodshed together." Jews could not survive the ravages of their own internal discord.

Sinat hinam was not a novel concept in Judaism. It had already been understood in Jewish tradition as a source of domestic friction — one of several relatively minor forms of "inappropriate behavior" within a family, along with mockery, vulgarity, and idleness. But some time after the destruction of the Second Temple, rabbis transformed *sinat hinam* into the ominous, and overriding, explanation for the *hurban*, the national calamity that had befallen the Jewish people. It had condemned them to exile from their holiest city and, ultimately, from their homeland. Over many centuries, Jews were taught to understand that the magnificent Temple, the religious and symbolic center of Jewish life, was destroyed not by Roman military power but by internecine Jewish conflict.

The rabbis who compiled Tractate *Yoma* (9b) of the Talmud, citing the dangers of *sinat hinam*, had not been alive to witness its destruction. But one of their distinguished forebears, Rabbi Yohanan ben Zakkai, was believed to have anticipated the impending catastrophe and planned for the survival of his people without a nation to sustain them. As the fighting and discord spread through Jerusalem, he had himself smuggled out of the city, with the collusion of his students, in a coffin. Once safely beyond the walls, its lid was opened and the rabbi arose to proclaim to Vespasian, the astonished Roman general: *"Vive domine imperator."* Flattered by Yohanan ben Zakkai's prophecy, Vespasian granted his wish for a place in Yavneh, a village near the Mediterranean coast, "where I might go and teach my disciples, and there establish a prayer house, and perform all the commandments."

In the absence of national sovereignty, the Yavneh academy molded rabbinic law as the primary instrument of Jewish autonomy and survival. Without royal, priestly or military authority, rabbinic interpretation of Torah was implanted within Jewish communities in exile. As harshly as Rabbi Yohanan ben Zakkai may be judged for his unseemly flight from Jerusalem, his shrewd — or desperate — acceptance of rabbinical authority as the necessary alternative to political sovereignty is credited with enabling the Jewish people to transcend their national catastrophe. In the void left by the destruction of the Second Temple, military defeat, national disintegration and exile, rabbis who followed the model of Yohanan ben Zakkai guided Jews from the zeal of force to the zeal of faith, leading them — in Jacob Neusner's apt phrase — "from politics to piety." So Jewish capitulation was transformed into Jewish triumph.

For nearly two thousand years, rabbinical legal authority, based on study of the Torah, Talmud and other religious texts, endured as the primary instrument of Jewish survival. These historical and religious sources justified the defeat of their people (and surrender to their conquerors) as the expression of divine will. But memories of the disaster in 70 CE, embedded in the historical narrative of Flavius Josephus and converging with rabbinical admonitions against *sinat hinam*, never disappeared.

Nineteen centuries later, secular European Zionists who rejected rabbinical authority helped to ignite the modern struggle for Jewish statehood. Rebelling against religious Orthodoxy and the political passivity that accompanied it, no less than the precariousness of diaspora existence amid persecution and pogroms, Zionists drew vital lessons from Jewish antiquity. Inspired by the military heroism of the Maccabees, Zealots, and Bar Kokhba — legendary ancient fighters for freedom from foreign domination — Zionists forged the struggle to restore national sovereignty in the lost homeland of their fabled ancestors. In memory, writes Israeli scholar Yael Zerubavel, antiquity was transformed into "the nation's golden age, the period to which the Zionists wished to return to recover their lost national roots."

Poet Yaakov Cahan, who composed *"Shir Ha-biryonim"* at the end of the 19th century, converted the 1st century Zealots, who had been condemned by Josephus for their fanatical zeal, into a vital source of modern inspiration:

> We arose, returned, we, the *biryonim*!
>
> We came to redeem our oppressed land
>
> . . .
>
> In blood and fire did Judaea fall;
>
> In blood and fire shall Judaea rise.

Long excoriated as reckless and destructive extremists, the ancient Zealots were recast by young Zionists as national heroes who inspired the national revolution that they dreamed of emulating.

Masada might seem to be an implausible place for constructing a national model for heroic behavior. Yet decades before the discoveries, lectures and writings that made archeologist Yigael Yadin a household name in Israel, intrepid Zionist pioneers had made hazardous pilgrimages through the desert and mountains of Judea to the ancient fortress ruins. In Yitzhak Lamdan's poem "Masada" (1927), the site became the powerful inspiration that could transport Zionists from defeat and exile to national restoration. The Masada pilgrimage became a Zionist rite of passage (for yeshiva students in Jerusalem no less than for Palmach fighters) from exilic helplessness to the remembered glory of ancient history and identity in the Jewish homeland.

Once young Zionists reached the Masada summit, they listened raptly to a reading of Josephus's haunting account of the fate — and courage — of the suicidal Zealots (as this writer did on his first trip to Israel nearly forty years ago). After Auschwitz, Zerubavel observes, Masada entered "secular national Hebrew culture as a counter-Holocaust metaphor." There, at least, Jews had not gone passively like sheep to the slaughter, the classic Zionist slur against pogrom and Holocaust victims alike. So, in the post-Holocaust era, Masada became "the glorification of patriotic death."

To pre-state Zionists, Jerusalem — spiritual home to endless generations of Jews who always remembered (especially at their Passover Seder) that they must not forget their ancient holy city — was of little interest. It did not, after all, inspire visions of suicidal heroism. Indeed, once secular Zionist nationalism replaced Jewish religious study and observance, Jerusalem yielded its place of primacy in Zionist symbolic significance, Zerubavel writes, to "the ruins of a fortress in the Judean desert."

The tragic finale to the Roman war at Masada, at least as recounted by Josephus, would do more to shape Zionist consciousness and Israeli collective memory than any other single episode in two millennia of Jewish history. The Zionist movement nurtured, and the young Jewish state cultivated, what one scholar has called "a series of deceptive and very biased (even falsified) claims" about Masada that transformed it into "a central symbol of heroism." In time, induction ceremonies were held at Masada for young soldiers who pledged their allegiance to the State of Israel. Their link to Jewish antiquity, a military brochure proclaimed, was "inextricable, undeniable, unbroken."

The Josephus narrative was hardly compatible with the heroic "new Jew" of Zionist mythology. Yet it fed the zeal of Zionist national renewal and was easily integrated into the continuing celebration of statehood and virtues of military preparedness. So Israeli soldiers were taught to draw courage and strength from an act of collective murder, as recounted by a Jewish military commander who had betrayed his nation to join its enemy when its very existence hung in the balance.

To Yigael Yadin, writing of his discoveries at Masada, "it seems evident that [Josephus] had been genuinely overwhelmed by the record of heroism on the part of the people he had forsaken." For the reknowned archeologist, the ancient defenders of Masada remained "Zealot Jews who fought for freedom" and "died for *Kiddush ha-*

Shem" (sanctification of God's name). It went all but unnoticed that the celebration of mass murder (capped by suicide) was a curious model for Zionist military heroism.

After the Six-Day War in 1967, the Masada myth began to deteriorate as a source of national inspiration. Scholars and intellectuals in Israel and the diaspora developed an "anti-heroic" critique of Masada. In time, among a younger generation of Israelis wearied and depleted by war, the Yom Kippur and Lebanon wars recast the Masada "complex," like the Bar Kokhba "syndrome" of misguided militarism, as a highly destructive form of political pathology, leading inevitably to spiritual, and even national, self-destruction.

Fed by deepening secular Zionist hostility to the pioneering religious settlers in biblical Judea and Samaria (the West Bank) after the Six-Day War, Masada became more of a tourist attraction than a Zionist shrine. Settlers were denounced as the newest "Zealots" (now a term of opprobrium) who would propel Israel, once again, into a destructive and futile war with its enemies, if not a civil war among Jews. Once Zionists on the religious right embraced national historical symbols that secular Zionists on the left had long cherished, the ideological primacy of the Josephus narrative gradually diminished. The new critique, the monopoly of "academics and political activists on the Left" (as Zerubavel indicates), became the conventional Israeli wisdom.

The application of ancient analogies, drawn from historical sources of questionable reliability and applied by modern Israelis with their own partisan axes to grind, is fraught with problems. Yet in a country separated from its periods of national existence by two thousand years of diaspora life, ancient precedents — whether real, imagined, or constructed — can still carry considerable, if sharply contested, ideological and political significance. Indeed, a mere six weeks after the proclamation of Israeli independence, Zionist discord erupted in fratricidal violence. With the arrival of the *Altalena*, ancient memories and modern politics suddenly converged. In

BROTHERS AT WAR

June 1948, the ominous danger of groundless hatred between Jews hovered once again over the Land of Israel.

Chapter 2
Conflict in Zion

The destruction of Jerusalem and its Temple in 70 CE became a seminal moment in Judaism. So, too, did the emergence of the Zionist movement eighteen centuries later. Precisely as Theodor Herzl had anticipated, the First Zionist Congress that convened in Basel in 1897 prepared the way for the rebirth of a Jewish state in fifty years. Yet just as ancient Jerusalem had been torn apart by conflict between rival Jewish sects while Roman legions encircled the city, so modern Zionists have occasionally been inclined to disregard the perils of "groundless hatred." Embracing the heroic struggles of their ancient heroes for national freedom, Zionists occasionally found it as difficult to live in peace with their own political rivals as did the ancestors whose memory they cherished.

Lord James Balfour's letter of November 2, 1917, known to history as the Balfour Declaration, conveyed the approval of the British government for "the establishment in Palestine of a national home for the Jewish people." It was affirmed in international law three years later at the San Remo Conference and in the League of Nations Mandate for Palestine, comprising the present day Kingdom of Jordan and all the land between the Jordan River and the Mediterranean. The Mandate assigned responsibility to Great Britain "for placing the country under such political, administrative and economic conditions as will secure the establishment of the Jewish National Home."

Under the terms of the Mandate, Great Britain was permitted to withhold application of its provisions from territory east of the Jordan River (comprising two-thirds of Palestine). Accordingly, in 1923 Colonial Secretary Winston Churchill designated that land as "Trans-Jordan," assigning it to Abdullah, son of the Emir of Mecca, for an independent kingdom. But the right of Jews to "close settlement" in truncated Palestine west of the Jordan River was protected in Article 6 (and has never been abrogated).

BROTHERS AT WAR

This first partition of Palestine, now long forgotten and disregarded even by most Israelis, instantly stripped Jews of two-thirds of their promised "national homeland." Yet it nonetheless contained the seeds of enduring conflict over the remaining territory of Palestine, not only between Jews and Arabs but since 1967 among Jews. It was not long before the Mufti of Jerusalem, Haj Amin al-Husseini, incited murderous Muslim violence toward Jews even within their truncated homeland. In 1929 the Mufti's followers in Jerusalem targeted Jews praying at the Western Wall, claiming as Muslim sacred space the remnant of the Second Temple enclosure that had been a Jewish holy site ever since its destruction, seven centuries before the birth of Islam. Violence quickly spread through Palestine, from Jerusalem to Tel Aviv, Safed and Tiberias. In the ancient city of Hebron, location of the revered Jewish holy site that marked the burial places of their biblical patriarchs and matriarchs, sixty-seven religious Jews — few of whom identified with Zionism — were brutally murdered in an Arab orgy of mutilation, rape, and torture.

The ineptitude of British military officials, who did little to contain the widespread violence and bloodshed, spurred the Yishuv, the Jewish community in Palestine, into action. The Haganah was organized as a paramilitary force to protect Jews against future attacks. Right-wing leader Vladimir (Ze'ev) Jabotinsky advocated the "revision" of Labor Zionist precepts to include the use of force, if necessary, to secure a Jewish state within the original Mandatory boundaries of Palestine, east and west of the Jordan River. Following the bloody pogroms of 1929, the Irgun (also known as Etzel) split off from the Haganah to implement Jabotinsky's demand for an "iron wall" of military power to resist Arab aggression.

In Mandatory Palestine, Labor and Revisionist leaders alike — David Ben-Gurion, Jabotinsky and his successor Menachem Begin — had been molded by political extremes, either left or right, in their native cultures in Poland and Russia. Quite aside from their divergent — ultimately irreconcilable — responses to British rule, the Revisionist vision of a middle-class society grounded in entrepreneurial freedom challenged the Labor Zionist dream of a socialist utopia, with kibbutzim as the model for Jewish national renewal. In the hothouse of Zionist politics in Palestine, set against the rise to power of Adolf Hitler in Germany, it did not take long before these ideological polarities fractured the Jewish community.

During the perilous journey to statehood, Labor and Revisionist Zionists clashed — sometimes violently — over divergent strategies for achieving national independence. In June 1933 a murder on the beach north of Tel Aviv ignited enmity between these Zionist political rivals that would reach its tragic climax fifteen years later, when the *Altalena* arrived in Israel.

Chaim Arlosoroff, a rising leader in the Mapai party that dominated the ruling Labor Zionist political coalition, had moved to Palestine a decade earlier after receiving his doctorate at the University of Berlin. To his astonishment, he encountered there what he described as a "massive nation" of Arabs. This perception indelibly molded his vision of the Zionist future: "We have only one way: the road of peace; only one national policy: a policy of mutual understanding."

Arlosoroff became political secretary of the Jewish Agency, the governing body of the Yishuv. To facilitate Arab-Jewish "co-existence," he strongly advocated "narrowing down the geographical area" of Zionist autonomy in Palestine. After the devastating riots in 1929, he began to meet with Arab moderates in an attempt to develop a bi-national movement of Arabs and Jews as an alternative to Jewish statehood.

In June 1933, Arlosoroff traveled to Germany as the representative of the Jewish Agency to negotiate an agreement with the new Nazi regime. It permitted Jews to immigrate to Palestine with some financial resources. But their substantial remaining assets would be transferred to the German government for the purchase and shipment of raw materials, chemicals, fertilizer, and iron to Palestine. The result, Arlosoroff believed, would be mutually beneficial to German Jews, Nazis and Palestinian Zionists. The safe departure of Jews from Germany would be assured; the Third Reich, already confronting a worldwide trade boycott by Jewish organizations, would enjoy a profitable market for exports to Palestine; and the Zionist economy would benefit from the flow of Jewish capital and German goods (purchased with Jewish money). Responding in a "top secret" memo to sharp criticism of his negotiations with the Nazi regime, Arlosoroff castigated the misguided "sentimentality" of his critics.

But as word of the transfer agreement spread, Arlosoroff was berated in Revisionist circles. Abba Ahimeir, leader of Brit Habirionim (a right-wing faction that adopted the name, if not the tactics, of 1st century Zealots) and editor of the newspaper *Hazit Haam*, accused him of "putting a knife in the back of the Jewish people while attempting to stretch out the hand of friendship to the Hitler government." The nation's honor, he charged, "had been sold to Hitler for a whore's wages."

In a pamphlet entitled "Manifesto of the Sicarii," Ahimeir warned that those who colluded with the "Roman enemy" might once again meet their fate at the hands of Jewish assassins. Brit Habirionim denounced Arlosoroff's transfer agreement with Nazis as a "pact with the devil." Even among mainstream Labor Zionist leaders, there was concern lest Arlosoroff's back-door negotiations with Nazi officials undermine their own political credibility in Palestine.

Arlosoroff returned from Germany to his Tel Aviv home on June 14. Two days later, *Hazit Haam* once again sharply criticized the alliance between the Labor Zionist Mapai party and Hitler: "There will be no forgiveness for those who have for greed sold out the honor of their people to madmen and anti-Semites." The Jewish people, Achimeir's newspaper proclaimed ominously, knew how to respond to "betrayers of the nation."

That Friday evening, after dinner, Arlosoroff and his wife Sima walked along the beach north of Tel Aviv. She noticed two men following them, but her husband reassured her that they were Jews. Near a Muslim cemetery on the outskirts of the city, they were stopped. One man shined a flashlight in Arlosoroff's face and asked, in fractured Hebrew, for the correct time. The other shot him with a Browning automatic pistol. Both men fled. Sima screamed: "Jews shot him." Her husband responded: "No, Sima, no." Several hours later, before Arlosoroff died in Hadassah Hospital, he repeated to a visitor that his assassins were not Jews.

His murder triggered the question that has yet to be conclusively answered: who killed Arlosoroff? Was it a Revisionist? An Arab nationalist? A British agent? Some even blamed Nazi propaganda minister Joseph Goebbels, whose wife Magda had been Arlosoroff's childhood friend. Police arrested two Arabs who confessed to the murder. But from a photograph (and, perhaps, police pressure), his widow identified Avraham Stavsky, an activist in the Revisionist Zionist youth organization Betar, as the man who held the flashlight, and Tzvi Rosenblatt, another Polish Revisionist, as Arlosoroff's assassin. Amid a surging wave of vitriolic political accusations and recriminations, police arrested both men along with journalist Abba Ahimeir, claiming that he was the mastermind of the assassination plot.

The Arlosoroff criminal investigation quickly became a legal travesty, laced with allegations of purchased confessions, false witnesses, and manufactured evidence. The Arabs who had confessed to the killing recanted. Tried for murder by a court comprising two British judges (one of whom was Jewish) and an Arab, Ahimeir and Rosenblatt were acquitted, while Stavsky's conviction and death sentence were overturned on appeal for insufficient evidence.

Although culpability for Arlosoroff's murder was never established, Labor party politicians remained convinced of right-wing guilt. Its leaders, and their faithful journalist allies, launched what political scientist Ehud Sprinzak has described as "an unprecedented delegitimation of the Revisionist movement . . . as fascist and terrorist." Ben-Gurion, leader of the party that had sent Arlosoroff to negotiate with Nazi Germany, referred to Jabotinsky as "Vladimir Hitler."

Many years later, the police inspector (a Haganah member) who had conducted the original investigation, accused British officials, with Haganah and Mapai collusion, of falsely blaming the Revisionists. In 1982 Prime Minister Menachem Begin established an Israeli investigating committee, led by a former Supreme Court Justice, to reexamine the still unresolved murder. It concluded that Stavsky and Rosenblatt were innocent of the crime; furthermore, there was no evidence that the murder of Arlosoroff had been politically motivated.

The transfer agreement (*haavara*) that Arlosoroff negotiated brought 20,000 Jews and $30 million to Palestine, along with $100 million in exports from Germany. Saving so many lives can hardly be dismissed as misguided or immoral. But neither could the consequences of negotiations between Palestinian Zionist officials and representatives of the Nazi government be casually disregarded. Undermining a global anti-Nazi boycott, they significantly strengthened the German economy.

The transfer agreement was an excruciating moral bargain that proved too painful for open discussion among Zionists at the time, and for years thereafter. To have ignored the opportunity of rescuing Jews was inconceivable. But Zionist negotiators could not provide the Nazi regime with desperately needed financial assistance and emerge with clean hands and their integrity intact. To the Zionist right, collaboration with the Nazi government was a heinous act; to the Zionist left, the murder of Arlosoroff exposed its political opponents as fascists and terrorists.

The Arlosoroff murder, and the highly politicized procedures and trials that followed in its aftermath, became the prelude to persistent internal Zionist conflict during the Mandatory era. The Arab revolt in 1936, spreading violence and terrorism throughout Palestine, reignited the smoldering hostility between rival Zionist factions. The Haganah was committed to a policy of *havlaga* (restraint), which did not satisfy more militant Zionists. By the end of 1937 Revisionist leaders were demanding *ayin tachat ayin* (the biblical admonition of "an eye for an eye"). Unconcerned with presenting a benign face to ruling British authorities, the Irgun fought Arab terror with Jewish terror, attacking Arab buses and cars and placing lethal explosives in civilian Arab neighborhoods.

In an attempt to quell the violence in Palestine the British Peel Commission recommended another partition, with two states west of the Jordan River. The plan was denounced by Revisionist Zionists, who decried the destruction of the territorial integrity of the historic land of Israel as a "treasonable conspiracy." Then, in 1939, the British government issued its notorious White Paper, reducing Jewish immigration to Palestine to a monthly trickle. Its accompanying recommendation for a single state with an Arab majority was a blatant betrayal of its Mandatory obligations and a devastating blow to the Zionist cause.

British willingness to appease Arabs in Palestine, precisely as the noose of annihilation was tightening around European Jews, propelled the Irgun into action. Redirecting their violent attacks from Arab to British targets, they bombed military bases and killed army officers. Whether this was anti-British "terrorism," as its left-wing opponents labeled it, or justified retaliation against a policy that would doom the Jews of Europe — no less than the prospect of Jewish statehood — the toxic mix of British appeasement, Irgun militancy, and Haganah restraint drove another deep wedge into the Zionist movement.

Yet even the Irgun response was insufficient for its own militant extremists. By 1940 a splinter faction, known as Lehi, had emerged under the leadership of Avraham Stern. It launched indiscriminate reprisals for Arab violence and continued its anti-British actions after the Irgun halted theirs. But during the early years of World War II a precarious truce prevailed among rival Jewish political factions in Palestine. The Irgun cooperated with Great Britain, even in joint military actions. Its commander, David Raziel, was killed on such a secret mission in 1941.

But three years later the Irgun was once again prepared to resist British rule in Palestine, by force if necessary. "The British regime has sealed its shameful betrayal of the Jewish people," it proclaimed, "and there is no moral basis whatsoever for its presence in Eretz

Israel." Rejecting Ben-Gurion's policy of self-restraint, it demanded the immediate transfer of British power to "a Provisional Hebrew Government." But before that happened, Menachem Begin anticipated, "we would have to carry out many operations. There would be suffering and we would be hounded incessantly."

An increasingly fierce opponent of British rule in Palestine, Begin was no less infuriated by Ben-Gurion's policy of cooperation — some alleged collaboration — with Mandatory authorities. While Nazis slaughtered Jews by the millions in Europe, the British government strictly adhered to its immigration restriction policy for Palestine. In February 1944, two months after he became commander of the Irgun, Begin issued a "Declaration of Revolt." Provoked beyond endurance by Ben-Gurion's deference to Great Britain, he decided that the time had come "to break through the gates from within" and fight for independence. "Our people is at war with this regime — war to the end."

But Ben-Gurion remained steadfastly convinced that cooperation with the British government would be more effective and cost fewer Jewish lives. It would also build international support that would be necessary for Jewish statehood once the war in Europe ended. He wanted to persuade the British — and other Western governments — that Palestinian Jews, unlike their Arab neighbors, were "a civilized community and a reliable ally."

Urged by some Irgun officers to retaliate against their Zionist political enemies, Begin responded: "I will never lend a hand to a war of brothers." Instead he focused his attention on the British, convinced that they would not leave until they were driven out. Attacks against the centers of Mandatory power in Palestine were, therefore, necessary and must continue. Lehi, the right-wing splinter faction, remained unrelenting in its commitment to violence in the struggle for Jewish statehood. Becoming, in effect, an "anti-British terrorist underground," it even explored the possibility of collaboration with the Nazi regime — precisely as Arlosoroff and his Mapai party had done a decade earlier.

CONFLICT IN ZION

The tenuous alliance between Zionist left and right had begun to unravel. Tension mounted on the left between the Haganah and the Palmach, its elite fighting force, and on the right between the Irgun and its breakaway Lehi faction. Haganah commander Eliahu Golomb declared publicly: "The dissident organizations are causing untold damage to Zionist diplomacy. . . . If there is no alternative, we will have to fight against these crazy and damaging actions."

Soon afterward, Ben-Gurion sent an emissary, Dr. Moshe Sneh — Haganah commander and member of the Jewish Agency — to try to persuade Begin to moderate his policy. In a five-hour meeting in October, Sneh emphasized the importance of international support for the Zionist struggle and the dangers of alienating the British government. Begin (who made "a pathetic impression" on Sneh) was not persuaded. Recognizing Ben-Gurion as the leader of the Yishuv, he would accept Ben-Gurion's command only "when he begins the war against the [British] government." At a second meeting several weeks later, Sneh — joined by Golomb — emphatically reminded Begin that the Provisional Government was the only democratically elected leadership and demanded the cessation of military operations. In the presence of Eliahu Lankin, Begin's trusted associate, Golomb warned that the government was prepared to end Irgun operations "at all costs."

Begin was not deterred. The Irgun underground, he wrote in his memoir (*The Revolt*), "arose to overthrow and replace a [British] regime. We used physical force because we were faced by physical force." But, he firmly insisted, there would be no civil war among Jews: "we did not teach the Irgun fighters to hate our political opponents. . . . As to who would ultimately rule the State . . . — that was unimportant." Ben-Gurion, determined to build the foundation for statehood without fighting the British, warned against "mad actions" that could destroy Zionism from within. But "if there is to be no alternative," he warned, "we shall face force with force." Soon afterward the Zionist government deported 251 Irgun fighters to Eritrea.

BROTHERS AT WAR

One month later two Lehi agents, enraged by British rule in Palestine and determined to avenge the murder of their leader Avraham Stern by British police two years earlier, assassinated Minister of State Lord Moyne in Cairo. Labor party leaders, unwilling to provoke conflict with the British and eager not to be equated with Lehi, condemned the murder and pursued what Ben-Gurion called "controlled" cooperation with British authorities. The choice, he asserted, was between "Zionist political struggle" and "terrorism." Chaim Weizmann, president of the World Zionist Organization and a loyal defender of British policy in Palestine, hastened to assure Prime Minister Winston Churchill, who had railed against "a new set of [Jewish] gangsters worthy of Nazi Germany" after Moyne's assassination, that Palestinian Jewry "will go the utmost limit of its power to cut out this evil from its midst."

Taking a harder line after the Moyne assassination, Ben-Gurion lacerated Jewish "criminals who endanger our future." He urged the Yishuv "to cast out all members of this underground gang" and pledged Labor Zionist cooperation with British authorities in "disgorging" terror. Golomb described a struggle between "Zionist democracy" and "Jewish Naziism." The *Histadrut*, the Zionist Labor federation, approved a policy of collaboration with British authorities to stifle its Irgun opponents. But within the Jewish Agency there were dissenters from the turn toward punitive retaliation against fellow Jews. Rabbi Fishman-Maimon of the religious Mizrahi party, and Yitzhak Gruenbaum of the General Zionist party, resigned from the executive committee in protest. Gruenbaum labeled collaboration with the British against fellow Zionists "the greatest tragedy" for the Zionist movement.

Determined that his own policy must prevail, Ben-Gurion launched the notorious *"Saison,"* the hunting season, to pursue and arrest Irgun leaders. It was necessary to act, he asserted, "not just to talk." The Season triggered what Begin described as "an all out crusade by Haganah and the Jewish Agency for our destruction." As Jews turned against Jews, angry words provoked hostile acts. It was a time, Sprinzak concluded, of "unprecedented Jewish collaboration with the British against other Jews." Once Lehi, solely responsible for the Moyne assassination, agreed to suspend its violent operations, the Irgun became the exclusive target of Labor Zionist wrath — and retaliation. Begin responded by instructing his Irgun followers: "There shall not be a war of brothers."

Nearly two hundred Palmach soldiers spearheaded the fight against Irgun dissidents, whose leaders were abducted and incarcerated in caves or kibbutzim. There they were interrogated, and occasionally tortured, before being turned over to British authorities. The Jewish Agency intelligence service and the Haganah cooperated as informants for the Palestinian police and British Secret Service against their right-wing opponents. The names of hundreds of Irgun members, Weizmann informed Churchill, were passed along to British authorities. It was, wrote Israeli journalist (and Begin biographer) Eitan Haber, "the darkest hour in Israel's battle for independence." Determined to fight the British, not other Jews, the Irgun refrained from retaliation. "Not civil war," Begin insisted. "Not that at any price."

From November 1944 until the following March, "hunting brothers" (the haunting subtitle of Yehuda Lapidot's book *Season*) remained Labor Zionist policy. Begin, disguised as an Orthodox rabbi named Israel Sassover, went into hiding in a quiet residential neighborhood in Tel Aviv. Having learned from his reading of Josephus both the danger of Roman military oppression (with which he equated British rule) and the terrible consequences of Jewish fratricide, the Irgun leader counseled restraint. He instructed his loyal fighters that regardless of the "terrible crime" inflicted against them by their Labor Zionist opponents, they must not retaliate. They obeyed their leader.

But in a proclamation drafted by Begin for public posting, the Irgun warned: "We Shall Repay You, Cain." In raging fury, it declared: "You rampage, Cain, . . . not to war for freedom, but for war of brother against brother." While Jews were being slaughtered by the Nazis, and Palestine was closed by the British government to desperate Jewish refugees, "you chose yourself an ally, Cain: the oppressive regime in the homeland." Begin's bitter indictment followed: "You incite, inform, betray, abduct, and hand men over, Cain." When it ended, he warned, "Cain" would be judged with "German murderers" and English "betrayers."

The Season proved to be "a dismal triumph" for Ben-Gurion (in the words of biographer Michael Bar-Zohar), leaving "open wounds" and "blinding hatred" in its wake. The collaboration of his government with British police and soldiers against the Irgun, Sprinzak writes, "left a deep scar in the Israeli collective memory," covering a wound that never fully healed. Irgun restraint during the Season, he concluded, represented "one of Menachem Begin's finest moments."

By the end of World War II, as the unimaginable horrors of the Holocaust were revealed, draconian British immigration restrictions — in place ever since the 1939 White Paper — reunited Palestinian Jews across their political divide. A United Resistance Movement was formed, comprising the Haganah, Irgun, and Lehi. But their brief period of unity lasted only until July 1946, when the Irgun — in its most spectacular attack against the Mandatory regime — blew up a wing of the King David Hotel in Jerusalem, headquarters of the British administration in Palestine. Despite advance warnings to evacuate the building, nearly one hundred civilians — mostly British, but also Arabs and Jews — were killed.

Although Haganah commander Moshe Sneh had participated in the planning and ordered the attack, the Haganah — uninformed of its precise timing — immediately condemned it. British outrage impelled Ben-Gurion to disband the United Resistance Movement. His loathing of Begin, and the "terrorist mindset" of his Irgun "thugs and terrorists," rekindled internecine Zionist hostility. The Irgun was dispatched into political and moral exile, beyond the pale of Zionist legitimacy.

Despite their acrimonious political differences, the Zionist left and right had long agreed upon the urgency of bringing Jewish refugees from Europe to Palestine to strengthen the Yishuv in its struggle for independence. The rickety ships that transported them were purchased and provisioned by Aliyah Beth, the underground branch of the Jewish Agency, and by Revisionist agents in the United States. Their rescue missions were repeatedly stymied by virulent Arab hostility to Jewish immigration, reinforced by British capitulation to Arab demands. But once World War II ended, Zionists were determined to open Palestine to Jewish survivors and rebuild a state in their ancient land.

Tens of thousands of homeless Jewish refugees, who were finally liberated from the extermination camps where millions had perished, awaited decisions by British authorities and the United Nations about their fate. Quietly and steadily, the flow of illegal immigration to Palestine resumed. But early in 1947, the British Secret Intelligence Service (MI6) was instructed by the Labour government to pursue clandestine "intimidation" that would lead to "unpleasant consequences" for refugeee ships. It launched "Operation Embarrass" to prevent Jews from leaving Europe for Palestine. Bombs were exploded in five ships docked in Italian ports; one was completely destroyed. A potential target was the *President Warfield*, soon to become known to the world as the *Exodus*.

Disregarding British quotas and intimidation, nearly fifty ships packed with Jewish survivors had docked in Palestine by mid-1947. This illegal immigration, historian Aviva Halamish writes, "took advantage of the weakness of the strong and the power of the weak." On July 11, a once elegant Chesapeake Bay ferry named the *President Warfield*, which had been given new life as a British navy vessel during the D-Day invasion of Normandy, left Séte in southern France for Palestine. Purchased by American Friends of the Haganah for $50,000, it was one of nine American ships that transported 30,000 illegal immigrants to Palestine after the war — and destined to become the most famous.

First mate Bill Bernstein, an American merchant marine veteran who came on board for postwar adventure, discovered his Jewish identity along the way. As he wrote excitedly to his brother, "Our people have only one burning desire here, — ALIYAH BETH! The second deliverance to Eretz Israel. The first migration was supposedly the handiwork of God, the second one we fight for."

BROTHERS AT WAR

Packed with 4590 Holocaust survivors (including 655 children), the *President Warfield* was tracked by British navy vessels, determined to prevent the Jews on board from reaching Palestine. Twenty miles off shore, while still in international waters, it was intercepted and rammed by British destroyers. Sailors and marines stormed the ship, fighting a pitched battle with passengers who responded to tear gas and clubs by throwing potatoes and cans of food. Bernstein, wielding a fire extinguisher to repel British sailors from the wheelhouse, was clubbed repeatedly in the head, suffered a serious concussion, and died. Tzvi Yakubovich, an orphaned teen-age survivor of Buchenwald, and Mordechai Baumstein, a 23-year-old refugee from a displaced persons camp in Germany, were shot to death.

Over the strenuous objections of Captain "Ike" Aronowicz, Ben-Gurion ordered the battered ship to surrender and proceed to Haifa harbor. When it arrived on July 18, escorted by eight British warships, it proudly displayed a banner bearing its new name — *Exodus 1947*. The ship, wrote American journalist Ruth Gruber, "looked like a matchbox that had been splintered by a nutcracker." It became, and has remained ever since, a vivid symbol of Zionist yearning and British perfidy.

Early the next morning, under tight British military security, the thwarted refugees were transferred from the *Exodus* to three other ships, soon to be known as "floating concentration camps." The Haifa pier, Gruber wrote, "began to take on the noise and smell and animal tragedy of a Chicago slaughterhouse." *Exodus* passengers were told that their destination was nearby Cyprus, where 25,000 Jews already languished in detention camps, awaiting entry to Palestine. But the British government, determined to stifle Jewish immigration and punish those who attempted it, instructed the ships to return the refugees to their point of departure in southern France. Zionist officials in the Ben-Gurion government, unwilling to antagonize British authorities, remained passively aloof and publicly silent.

The poignant odyssey of the *Exodus* overlapped with another, far more violent, drama that was simultaneously unfolding in

Palestine. In April Dov Gruner, who had emigrated from Hungary in 1940 on an illegal immigrant ship, was brought to the gallows in Acre prison by his British captors. A member of Betar and then the Irgun, Gruner had joined the Jewish Brigade of the British army to fight against their common Nazi enemy. After the war ended, he returned to Palestine to enlist as a fighter for Jewish independence, participating in Irgun attacks against a British army depot near Netanya and a police station in Ramat Gan. Wounded, captured, imprisoned and brought to trial, he was sentenced to death.

Gruner addressed his final letter to his Irgun commander, Menachem Begin:

> There are many schools of thought as to how a Jew should choose his way of life. One way is that of the assimilationists who have renounced their Jewishness. There is also another way, the way of those who call themselves 'Zionists' — the way of negotiation and compromise, as if the existence of a nation were nothing but another transaction. . . . The only way that seems right, to my mind, is the way of the Irgun Zvai Leumi, the way of courage and daring without renouncing a single inch of our homeland. . . . For it is a law of history that only with blood shall a country be redeemed.

On April 19th, Gruner — along with three other Irgun fighters — was hanged in Acre prison. Each man, joined by the remaining others, sang *Hatikvah* until his death.

In a daring rescue attempt two weeks later, Irgun fighters disguised as British soldiers blasted open the gates and wall of Acre prison. Twenty-seven Irgun prisoners escaped, but British soldiers killed nine attackers and captured three others, who were quickly tried and sentenced to death. In a stunning act of retaliation on July 12, the day after the *Exodus* sailed from France to Palestine, the Irgun kidnapped two British sergeants and held them hostage pending the release of their own imprisoned fighters. Zionist leaders, stung by British fury and determined to stifle Irgun dissidents, instructed Haganah fighters to collaborate with the British in searching out their hiding places.

BROTHERS AT WAR

While three ships carrying *Exodus* refugees were returning to France, British High Commissioner Alan Cunningham ordered the three captured Irgun fighters to be hanged. Two days later, on July 29th, they died on the gallows. That morning, Irgun chief of staff Haim Landau ordered the retaliatory hanging of the British sergeants. Their booby-trapped bodies were discovered dangling from a tree in a eucalyptus grove outside Netanya.

Enraged British soldiers in Tel Aviv responded by attacking Jewish civilians, killing five and injuring fifteen. British Foreign Secretary Ernest Bevin declared that it would not surprise him "if the Germans had learned their worst atrocities from the Jews." Anti-Semitic rioting in England targeted synagogues and Jewish property. With its counter-insurgency strategy failing, and Irgun retaliation mounting, British authority in Palestine showed signs of unraveling.

As these dramatic events unfolded in Palestine, the *Exodus* refugees, comprising "a whole city of Jews . . . afloat in the prison ships," awaited their fate in Port-du-Bouc. Despite oppressive heat, privation, exhaustion and illness, the refugees refused to disembark, rejecting any destination but Palestine. French officials expressed surprise that Yishuv leaders "did nothing to prevent the British from deporting the immigrants." Tension surfaced between Haganah youth movement members on board, who favored passive resistance, and Irgun representatives who, they feared, "were likely to force us into activism, through some irresponsible act." A Zionist emissary on board one of the ships complained that the *Exodus* refugees "asked for one thing: that the Zionist movement and the Yishuv in Palestine stand by them, fight with them, and we promised them this." But no help came from Zionist officials in Palestine.

After three weeks of futile negotiations, and the refusal of passengers to leave, the ships finally sailed to Hamburg, where British soldiers forcibly removed and transported them to internment camps. Confined once again behind barbed wire in Germany, the *Exodus* refugees bore stark witness to the unraveling of British Mandatory authority and the vindictive anti-Semitism that accompanied it. The decision to return the refugees to Germany seemed gratuitously repulsive: it was, Halamish writes, "an inhumane and conscienceless toying with the pitiful remnants of the ghettoes and concentration camps." The British government, battered by criticism at home and abroad and exhausted by its struggle to suppress "terrorists in Palestine" (as opposition leader Winston Churchill labeled the Irgun), began to plan for its withdrawal.

By the summer of 1947, the moral bankruptcy of British rule in Palestine, the ordeal of the *Exodus*, and Irgun retribution against the British sergeants framed the struggle for Jewish statehood. So, too, did the unabated tension between rival Jewish political factions in Palestine. While the Jewish Agency quietly acquiesced in the deportation of refugees from the *Exodus*, consigning their fate to British hands without any discernible resistance, it excoriated the Irgun for kidnapping and killing the sergeants. To Moshe Shertok, head of its Political Department, the hanging was an "outrageous act" that brought "abysmal shame and disgrace" upon Zionism, diverting attention from the plight of the *Exodus* refugees — which the Jewish Agency had done virtually nothing to alleviate.

The Irgun and Lehi, in turn, lacerated "pathetic" and "traitorous" Zionist leaders and their "ghetto council." Irgun leader Hillel Kook berated the Jewish Agency for "betraying the *Exodus* immigrants by ordering them not to use force in resisting their removal from the deportation ships." A delegate to the Zionist General Council meeting in Zurich that summer complained that Zionist leaders "had placed the major burden on the weakest of shoulders — those of the immigrant. The Yishuv was not an active partner in the struggle." Yet violent Irgun resistance to British rule, so deplorable to Labor Zionists, seemed to be effective. After the hanging of the British sergeants, there were no further executions of Jewish fighters. Two months later, the British government announced its intention to relinquish its Mandate and withdraw from Palestine.

To Ben-Gurion, the Irgun — not the British — had long been the more dangerous enemy. The Jewish Agency, under his leadership since 1935 and eager to be recognized as the legitimate Zionist governing authority in Palestine, was rarely willing to jeopardize relations with British authorities. But by the end of July 1947, the intertwining of the *Exodus* and the hangings of Irgun fighters brought the Yishuv to the edge of crisis. Helpless to protect the *Exodus* refugees, Jewish Agency officials could only blame Irgun "terrorists" for incurring the wrath of the world. They would demonstrate their strength, and assert control, by fighting the Irgun but not the British. It was a decision with haunting reverberations exactly one year later, when internal Zionist violence erupted in the confrontation over the *Altalena*.

Yet for a brief moment in May 1948, when the Jewish nation proclaimed its independence in its ancient homeland, reconciliation finally prevailed over discord. In the founding text of the old-new nation, potentially divisive differences were carefully camouflaged with ambiguity. Labor party preferences for territorial compromise clashed with right-wing yearning for "the greater land of Israel" within the borders of biblical Palestine. Consequently, the boundaries of the new state remained undefined.

Ben-Gurion, citing the American Declaration of Independence as a precedent for territorial vagueness, wrote: "A nation declaring its independence does not have to define its boundaries. We should say nothing about them because we don't know what they will be." The surging hostility of Israel's Arab neighbors, who rejected the United Nations partition agreement and were poised to annihilate a Jewish state within any borders, meant that boundaries would be decided by war, not by eloquent declarations.

"With trust in the Rock of Israel," the Proclamation of Independence declared in its concluding peroration, "we set our hand to this Declaration . . . in the city of Tel Aviv, on this Sabbath eve, the fifth of Iyar, 5708, the 14th day of May 1948." That single sentence, as literary scholar Harold Fisch astutely perceived, exposed the latent ambiguities of Jewish statehood that were rooted in the attempt to fuse ancient memories and modern yearnings, religious faith and secular convictions. The reference to "the Rock of Israel" (*Tzur Yisrael*) might refer either to God or to the collective national resolve of the Jewish people — or both. Over the opposition of secular members of the drafting committee, the elderly Rabbi Yehuda Lieb Fishman, a member of Ben-Gurion's Cabinet, had insisted upon its retention. His wish prevailed. The word "*betachon*" (immediately preceding *Tzur Yisrael)* also had a double meaning: (military) "security" and (religious) "faith." Linguistic ambiguity reflected dualities embedded within the Zionist dream at its very moment of fulfillment.

Although the borders of the new state were unclear, Tel Aviv was explicitly included within them. The enduring promise of Jews through the ages — to remember Jerusalem — was momentarily, but not accidentally, ignored. Designated for international status by the United Nations partition resolution, Jerusalem lay outside the boundaries allocated to the new Jewish state. (It was a decision that would have lingering reverberations, the following year, during negotiations over the *Altalena.*) In the end, even the dating of the Proclamation was ambiguous, revealing a nation that simultaneously embraced two measurements of time, separately marked by the Jewish and Christian calendars. Israel was unable — or unwilling — to choose between them. In time no less than space, the nascent state remained undefined.

At the signing ceremony just before the beginning of the Jewish Sabbath, Ben-Gurion — who, as Chairman of the Provisional Zionist Council, had read the Proclamation — announced that Rabbi Fishman, the oldest member of the Proclamation drafting committee, would recite the *Shehehiyanu*, the traditional Jewish prayer of thanksgiving. It was a generous gesture of honor to the elderly rabbi, and to the religious tradition that he symbolized. (During the prayer, however, Ben-Gurion remained bareheaded.) Then members of the Council signed the Proclamation and sang *Hatikvah* — expressing the transformative desire of a free people in its own land.

So, in the founding text of Jewish statehood, conflict over territorial boundaries was averted, at least temporarily, while the delicate balance between religion and state was, at least symbolically, preserved. But the sharp internal divisions between the

BROTHERS AT WAR

Zionist left and right that had wracked the Yishuv ever since the Arlosoroff murder remained a potent danger to the stability of the new nation. There were ominous uncertainties: Did statehood portend cohesion or conflict? Would independence mark the climax of national unity or trigger an eruption of groundless hatred? What legacy from antiquity, if any, did the newborn Jewish state inherit?

The next evening, Menachem Begin delivered a radio address to the nation in which he exulted in "the first Hebrew revolt since the Hasmonean [Maccabean] insurrection that has ended in victory." Begin acknowledged: "One phase of the battle for . . . the return of the whole people of Israel to its homeland, for the restoration of the whole Land of Israel to its God-covenanted owners, has ended." But, he reminded his listeners, it was "only one phase." The "truncation of the homeland," he declared, "is illegal. It will never be recognized."

Speaking to the *Histadrut* three days later, Ben-Gurion conceded: "Our land was reduced, Jerusalem was made an international city . . . and our borders are bad from a political and military standpoint." But, he proudly asserted, "there has never been a greater achievement than this." Indeed, the Jewish people once again had their own state in their promised land.

Who, then, were the Zealots in 1948? To build a state Labor Zionists had boldly rejected the Yavneh model of accommodation, study, and prayer that Rabbi Yohanan ben Zakkai had carefully crafted from the shattered remnants of national destruction. But who could claim the mantle of the Maccabees, echoing Mattathias's call: "Let everyone that is zealous for the Law and that would maintain the covenant come forth after me!" Who were the *sicarii*, the last desperate holdouts at Masada? Should they be celebrated as Zionist heroes — or condemned as Jewish terrorists? Who were the Hellenized Jews, targeted both by the Maccabees and the Zealots as traitors to the cause of Jewish national independence? In 1948 would Zionist freedom fighters, engaged in a desperate struggle for Jewish national independence, elude the destructive ancient peril of *sinat hinam*, or relive it?

CONFLICT IN ZION

At its moment of national birth, Israel was sufficiently vulnerable to imminent Arab invasion to trigger dire concerns among its political and military leaders about the viability of the new state. Just three days after independence was declared, with Arab armies poised to attack on its borders, Ben-Gurion asked Yigael Yadin, his Chief of Operations, whether Israel could survive for even two more weeks without a massive infusion of weapons from its overseas allies. Yadin, Ben-Gurion recorded tersely, "is not certain."

Not six weeks later, amid desperate Israeli attempts to obtain military supplies that could determine the fate of the Jewish nation, the long simmering conflict between Zionists on the left and right erupted into open warfare. Pitched battles at Kfar Vitkin, near Netanya, and then on the Tel Aviv beach, not far from the spot where Chaim Arlosoroff had been murdered fifteen years earlier, confronted Israel with an incipient civil war. At the center of the conflict was the *Altalena*.

Chapter 3
Civil War?

The story of the *Altalena* began on the eve of World War II, when six young Irgun loyalists who became known collectively as the Bergson Boys arrived in New York. Their leader, Hillel Kook, was the twenty-four year-old Lithuanian-born nephew of Rabbi Abraham Isaac HaCohen Kook, the Ashkenazi Chief Rabbi of Mandatory Palestine. Better known by his pseudonym Peter Bergson (adopted to avoid tainting the Kook family with his Revisionist politics), Kook and his partners devised an innovative public relations campaign to mobilize support and raise money for the rescue of European Jews and, after the war, for the establishment of a Jewish state. Bergson's "Boys," all in their twenties, included Yitzhaq Ben-Ami, Arieh Ben-Eliezer, and Alexander Rafaeli, joined soon after by Jabotinsky's son Eri and secretary Samuel Merlin.

The Bergson Boys have been aptly described as the "prototype of an American ethnic interest/protest group." At a time when American Jews were too insecure to assert identifiably Jewish interests lest they be accused of divided loyalty, these brash new arrivals — with experience forged in the hothouse of Zionist politics in Europe — were uninhibited by American Jewish anxieties and trepidations. Determined to shatter the silence surrounding the impending annihilation of European Jewry, they launched a cluster of organizations: the Committee for a Jewish Army, the Emergency Committee to Save the Jews of Europe, the American League for a Free Palestine and the Hebrew Committee for National Liberation. They funded illegal immigration into Palestine, the rescue of survivors once the war ended, and a Jewish army for the new state.

But to the American Jewish establishment, spanning the liberal American Jewish Congress led by Rabbi Stephen S. Wise and the conservative American Jewish Committee led by New York lawyer Joseph M. Proskauer, the Bergson Boys were "a military-fascist" group that had no place in American Jewish life. They were also anathema to the "President's Jews," members of Roosevelt's inner circle of advisers, for pressing the President to include the rescue of Jews in a war strategy that was indifferent, if not oblivious, to their imminent annihilation.

As early as February 1943, public rallies and newspaper advertisements focused attention on the desperate situation of European Jewry. Kook keenly appreciated the power of the media to shape public opinion in a democratic society. A dramatic pageant, "We Will Never Die," the collaboration of screenwriter Ben Hecht and composer Kurt Weill, attracted a rapt audience of supporters that filled Madison Square Garden in New York before leaving on tour to rally nation-wide support for the beleaguered Jews of Europe. At a time when the sound of silence surrounding the Holocaust framed government policy in Washington and paralyzed deferential American Jewish leaders, such passionate public expressions of support for European Jewry were exceedingly rare — and, to many Jews, unwelcome.

Once the war ended, the Bergson Boys shifted their focus and fund-raising efforts. Ships were desperately needed to transport Jewish refugees to Palestine in defiance of British restrictions. The American League for a Free Palestine purchased a 400-ton former yacht, the *S.S. Abril*, which sailed for France with a crew of American volunteers in December 1946. At Port-du-Bouc, six hundred Holocaust survivors boarded the ship, renamed the *S.S. Ben Hecht*, for the journey to Palestine. Ten miles from their destination, British destroyers intercepted the vessel. Jewish passengers were dispatched to a detention camp in Cyprus and members of the crew were incarcerated in Acre prison.

The Irgun persisted. Early in 1947, Yitzhaq Ben-Ami, a leader of the Hebrew Committee for National Liberation, met with Menachem Begin in Palestine to plan additional shipments of refugees and weapons. Upon his return to the United States Ben-Ami was contacted by Avraham Stavsky, the Revisionist activist who had been sentenced to death and then exonerated for the murder of

CIVIL WAR?

Arlosoroff. They negotiated the purchase of a 4,000-ton, diesel-powered LST-138 that had participated in the D-Day invasion.

Rescued from the mothballed American fleet on the Hudson River near West Point, the ship was moved to Gravesend in Brooklyn and named *Altalena*, once Jabotinsky's pen name (meaning "see-saw" in Italian). "We needed a name," explained Eliahu Lankin, commander of the Irgun in the Diaspora, "that would be understood by the friends of Zion while remaining obscure to the rest of the world." Stavsky recruited Monroe Fein, a 25-year-old Navy veteran from Chicago who answered an ad in a Chicago newspaper, to serve as captain. Fein had commanded a similar ship in the Pacific. He was, Lankin wrote, "an excellent seaman, intrepid, and . . . a Jewish patriot."

For nearly a year, while its sponsors struggled to obtain the necessary funding for the journey to Palestine, the *Altalena* marked time with a series of inconsequential voyages. It hauled potatoes from New Brunswick to Virginia and sailed to Florida for lumber. During the winter of 1947—48 it made stops in Cuba, Italy, France and Casablanca before returning to Europe to await authorization to depart for the nascent Jewish state.

But its planners confronted an unexpectedly complex challenge. Clandestine coordination with French government representatives was essential to supply the ship with weapons, facilitate the boarding of passengers, and authorize its departure from a French port. Secrecy was urgent lest the British navy enjoy yet another opportunity to seize a Jewish refugee ship and divert its passengers, as it had already done with the *Exodus* and the *Ben Hecht*. For the mission to have any chance of success, it was necessary to coordinate plans with Ben-Gurion's Provisional Government, which continued to view the Irgun with intense hostility and suspicion.

To the Irgun, the Zionist determination to build a Jewish state and the irrepressible longing of Jews for Jerusalem were inseparable. Ever since the Babylonian exile Jews had pledged: "If I forget thee, O Jerusalem, let my right hand forget her cunning / If I do not remember thee, let my tongue cleave to the roof of my mouth; if I prefer not Jerusalem above my chief joy." But following the United Nations resolution in November 1947 to partition Palestine, during the months preceding the termination of the British Mandate, Jerusalem tumbled into violent chaos.

The Jewish Quarter of the Old City, under unrelenting siege, was slowly strangled. Arab fighters blocked the roads; food supplies dwindled; water was severely rationed. It became an isolated enclave of privation, danger, and despair. By the spring of 1948, with British authority waning, conditions were dire. The Jordanian Arab Legion — highly trained (by the British) and amply provisioned with weapons — was poised for a final assault in the Old City, where fewer than two hundred meagerly armed Haganah and Irgun fighters were left to defend 1,500 desperate Jews. A Palmach relief brigade managed to enter through the Zion Gate, at the edge of the Quarter, with ammunition and medical supplies for the beleaguered fighters but it did not remain to defend the residents.

In mid-May, with the British departure and Jewish independence imminent, Ben-Gurion anticipated that the United Nations would relinquish its plan for the internationalization of Jerusalem and accede to the impending Arab conquest. He ordered David Shaltiel, the commander of Haganah forces in Jerusalem, to "attack and attack and attack." But the cautious Shaltiel hesitated. Lacking military command experience, and antagonistic toward to the Irgun from his time as a Haganah counter-intelligence officer, he felt bound by the decision of the Jewish Agency to accept internationalization. He was willing to abandon the Jewish Quarter, the better to concentrate his sparse forces in neighborhoods outside the Old City.

The final battle for the Quarter raged for ten days. Inside the besieged enclave, Jewish fighters — under-trained, scantily supplied, and randomly assembled from separate military and rival political units — comprised a motley but fiercely determined brigade. Avraham Weinfeld, an Irgun member who had been arrested as a suspect in the King David Hotel bombing, was sent there because he knew how to make bombs. Shaul Tawil, a schoolteacher in the

CIVIL WAR?

Quarter, had led a paramilitary youth group that trained youngsters for the Haganah. Leah Wiltz, who organized underground operations for the Irgun in the Old City, filled discarded Players cigarette tins with gunpowder, glass, nuts, bolts and matches while her husband, a talented cellist, delicately cut the detonators. Seventeen-year-old Uri Golani, sent into the Old City by the Haganah the previous November, operated a secret radio station for six months until the surrender. Leonard Binder, a Hebrew University student from Boston, never even got to see the Western Wall before he was captured and taken to Jordan as a prisoner of war.

By May, the unremitting fighting had driven hundreds of frantic Jewish residents to abandon their battered homes. With little food or water, no electricity, unable even to bury their dead (whose bodies were stacked outside the solitary medical clinic), they frantically sought refuge in the 16th century Yohanan ben Zakkai synagogue. Under relentless siege, the rabbinical leaders of the community counseled surrender. An explosion that destroyed the magnificent old Hurva synagogue foreshadowed the end, which finally came on May 28. Joseph Atich, an elementary school teacher and Palmach reservist, long remembered the desperate cries of *Sh'ma Yisrael* that resounded through the Jewish Quarter as the tragic climax neared. Only thirty-five battered Jewish fighters, without ammunition to sustain their struggle any longer, remained standing to surrender.

Photographer John Phillips, who spent eleven days in an Arab Legion uniform documenting the destruction of the Jewish Quarter, described it as "a charred and burned out shell." Driven from Jerusalem by Babylonians, Romans, Persians, Crusaders and now Muslims, the newest Jewish refugees were escorted through the Zion Gate while behind them marauding Arabs set their homes ablaze. "The smell of burning," recalled Phillips, who would return in 1975 to interview and photograph survivors for his splendid book, *A Will to Survive*, "mingled with the stench of death."

A final, futile attempt to retain the Old City for the new State of Israel came a month after the war for independence began. Just before the United Nations imposed a cease-fire to begin on June 11th, Shaltiel decided to blow open the Old City wall and send fighters from the Palmach, Irgun and Lehi in a desperate effort to regain the Jewish Quarter. In the plans for a coordinated assault, Irgun fighters would attack through the New Gate, Lehi would enter the Jaffa Gate, and Palmach soldiers would arrive through an opening blasted in the wall adjacent to Zion Gate. But the plan went awry when explosives failed to breach the wall. The Jewish Quarter was lost, but the Irgun had not abandoned hope of wresting ancient Jewish holy sites from their newest Arab conquerors.

On May 15th, the day after Israel declared independence, Menachem Begin delivered a radio address to the new nation. "Within the boundaries of the Hebrew independent state," he declared, "there is no need for a Hebrew underground. In the State of Israel, we shall be soldiers and builders. We shall respect its Government, for it is our Government." Outside the boundaries of the state, however, where "the homeland is not yet liberated," the Irgun would continue its military struggle. That meant Jerusalem. As Shmuel Katz, a member of the Irgun high command and a close adviser to Begin, wrote: "We never forgot Jerusalem, where the Israeli government refused to claim sovereignty."

At midnight, Begin and three members of the Irgun high command — Yaakov Meridor, Chaim Landau and Katz — met with Yisrael Galili, former head of the Haganah national command who had recently become Ben-Gurion's Deputy Defense Minister, accompanied by Levi Eshkol from the Ministry of Defense. Begin informed them that the Irgun had purchased an American naval ship. Once bureaucratic problems in France were resolved, it would bring to Israel hundreds of volunteers for the army and substantial supplies of weapons. Ben-Gurion's representatives did not object.

The next day Ben-Gurion, serving simultaneously as Prime Minister and Defense Minister in the Provisional Government, informed its members that due to the lack of rifles only 40% of Jewish military recruits could be armed. The situation, he warned, was "extremely serious." On May 26th, the government established the Israel Defense Forces as the army of the State of Israel and prohibited the "continued existence of any other armed force." The Irgun promptly announced that it would cease military operations inside the borders of the new state.

One week later, Begin met again with government and military officers, including Galili and Yigael Yadin, head of military operations, to coordinate the integration of Irgun military units into the new Israeli army. Its battalions would join the Israel Defense Forces, while remaining unified under their own commanders. It would turn over its military supplies to the IDF and refrain from separate weapons purchases. Nothing was explicitly stated about Jerusalem, where the Israeli government would not exercise sovereignty. Begin assumed the freedom of Irgun military units (along with Lehi and Palmach fighters) to continue to engage in battle there, beyond national borders. The agreement was signed on June 3rd.

Ever since February the *Altalena* had been sailing between Marseilles and Casablanca, awaiting its opportunity — contingent on funding, availability of weapons, the coordinated arrival of passengers and crew, and permission from the French government — to depart for Palestine. In Marseilles, diplomatic officials from various countries closely monitored its activities. The American Consul General notified the Secretary of State that "a converted Liberty ship flying the Panamanian flag" had arrived from Genoa. He appended a list of the crew and "data regarding each" member.

The local Panamanian consul boarded the ship and found it in "a lamentable state of sanitation, 'the dirtiest he had ever seen.'" Detecting no signs of adequate equipment for loading or handling cargo, he notified local police that it was "suspicious" and informed Captain Fein not to "attempt to engage in any improper activities if he expected to sail the vessel from this port." The consul, his American counterpart reported, "had in mind the Palestine situation." Haganah agents came on board to explore possibilities for supplementing the shipment with weapons for their own military forces. Negotiations were halted, Captain Fein recalled, after they received orders from Israel "to have nothing to do with the *Altalena*."

BROTHERS AT WAR

The Irgun commander in Europe responsible for coordinating the *Altalena* expedition was Eliahu Lankin. Born in Russia, he grew up in China and came to Palestine in 1933. Active in the Irgun, he was arrested by the British in 1944 and sent to a detention camp in Eritrea, from which he escaped. Based in Paris after the war, he scouted Europe for military supplies to sustain the struggle for Jewish independence.

By 1948, weapons had trickled in from Zionist supporters in Belgium, Sweden, Spain and France. French Communists and Spanish anarchists who had taken refuge in a French mountain village donated guns to the Irgun "freedom fighters." The Jewish Agency funded a substantial acquisition of Czech rifles. At Meridor's suggestion, a dozen volunteer pilots with wartime flying experience were mobilized to protect the ship on its journey to Palestine, but no planes could be located for the mission. With funds drawn from a Swiss bank account, arrangements were made to transport passengers from various European locations to southern France, where the *Altalena* awaited them.

The departure of the ship depended, in the end, on permission from the government of France. Without its cooperation, the *Altalena* would remain moored in Marseilles. Shmuel Ariel, a Romanian native who arrived in Paris after the war, had been working tirelessly as the Irgun's unofficial diplomatic representative, trying to secure French government support for the political objective that it shared with the Irgun: to drive the British from Palestine. Through a network of personal contacts, Ariel established relations with French government officials, especially in the Ministry of the Interior, who were receptive to his plan. But his lavish Parisian life style aroused suspicion among his more abstemious Irgun associates, resulting in his temporary suspension. With strong support from Lankin, Ariel was returned to favor and resumed his conspicuous socializing and clandestine negotiations.

In the name of the Irgun, Ariel presented a memorandum to the French Foreign Ministry in late March 1948 proposing a secret agreement between France and "a Hebrew Palestine as the Irgun envisages it." He had little to offer but the future good will of a still unborn Jewish state. But he claimed that a "free and powerful" Jewish Palestine would constitute an effective barrier against the expansionist objectives of the Arab League, while assuring France "significant freedom of action" in the Middle East. The Irgun requested a training base to be located in French "metropolitan or colonial territory," provisioned with sufficient military supplies — 5000 rifles, 250 machine guns, and 5 million rounds of ammunition — for a brigade of Jewish fighters to reach Palestine by May 15th.

The official ultimately responsible for the emerging alliance of mutual interest between the Irgun and the French government was Foreign Minister George Bidault. A Resistance leader during World War II, he was a strong proponent of the continued exercise of French colonial power in the Middle East, which British activity in Syria and Lebanon had severely undermined. In his clandestine diplomatic explorations Bidault had developed relations with both the Haganah and Irgun. The determination of the Irgun to expel Great Britain from Palestine, by force if necessary, proved decisive in gaining his support.

"In reality," Lankin subsequently conceded, "we had nothing to offer the French in return for their arms." But the Irgun could assure them that "these arms would be used to liberate our country from the tyranny of British rule and to defend ourselves from the invading Arab armies. If the fulfillment of this aim also harmed the prestige of France's traditional enemy, then we could only be grateful for this confluence of goals." In the end, that convergence of interests proved decisive.

The French decision to support the Irgun was driven by the "old Anglo-French rivalry." As Israeli scholar Meir Zamir has demonstrated, it involved a delicate balancing of French interests. Endorsement of a Jewish state ran the risk of stoking anti-French hostility among North African Muslims still under French colonial rule. But its establishment might hasten the British departure from Palestine. Zamir reveals that once British officials "openly supported the Arabs and sought to prevent the establishment of the Jewish state," warning that it would become "a center of communist influence" in the Middle East, the French government responded.

Arab military gains in Jerusalem during the waning weeks of the Mandate propelled Bidault to act. Viewing the Arab Legion as a British tool to preserve imperial control, French officials grew increasingly concerned over Arab attacks on Christian holy places, including the Notre Dame cathedral in Jerusalem. In early June, with war raging throughout the city, the French Consulate was shelled. If the British and Arabs were allies, then France would support the Irgun, whose determination to defend Jerusalem remained undiminished.

On May 29th the *Altalena* moved from Marseilles to nearby Port-du-Bouc. One week later, the French Minister of Armed Forces — as instructed by the Foreign Minister's office — signed a secret agreement with the Irgun. France would deliver the requested munitions, valued at more than 150 million francs. Described by a critical French official as a "war operation" conducted "outside any regular procedure," it was vaguely identified as a decision of the Government "for reasons of foreign policy."

French army trucks, driven by soldiers under the command of French army officers and loaded with military supplies, arrived in Port-du-Bouc. A Haganah representative in Paris informed Ben-Gurion by cable that the *Altalena* would be transporting immigrants and weapons. "It was my understanding," Captain Fein recalled, "that all preparations were being made with the full knowledge and acquiescence of the Israel government."

It was a joyously chaotic moment when the trucks arrived and passengers prepared for departure. Yeshayahu Warshaw enthusiastically described "a melting pot" of "fellows and girls from practically every important country in the world," awaiting the opportunity to board. An Italian contingent, uniformed in khaki with backpacks and field equipment, arrived from Milan. A group from Austria had been delayed in Linz until local officials could be persuaded to issue 250 visas to war refugees lacking any identification. Two hundred recruits from Germany smuggled crates of weapons and ammunition on board their train, crossing into France unimpeded once they shared bottles of cognac with border guards. Seventy-five men came from Czechoslovakia after months of military training in the Carpathian Mountains. Most of the Europeans were survivors of Nazi extermination camps; many had spent their postwar years confined to displaced persons camps. Aaron Green and Joe Kohn, assimilated American Jews from New York who had suddenly been galvanized by the struggle for Jewish statehood, were conspicuous exceptions.

The youngest passenger, born in Prague sixteen years earlier, was Pavel Friedländer. The son of parents whom he would describe as "typical representatives of the assimilated Jewish bourgeoisie of Central Europe," Friedländer had stronger childhood memories of visits to Prague churches than to the famous *Altneushul* or the adjacent centuries-old Jewish cemetery. With the outbreak of war, his family fled to Paris and, when the deportation of Jews began in 1942, to southern France. There, to assure their son's safety, his parents placed him in a Catholic boarding school. Renamed Paul-Henri, he "passed over to Catholicism body and soul" and yearned to become a priest.

The war ended but Friedländer's parents did not return. When he learned that they had been murdered in Auschwitz, he left school after the 7th grade to be placed with guardians in Paris. Their home, he recalled, was "saturated with Jewish emotions, allusions, customs, mannerisms." That summer he attended a Zionist camp run by the Habonim youth movement, where his new affinities for Communism and Zionism intersected. Inspired by the UN decision to establish a Jewish state, Friedländer decided to become a participant in the struggle: "How could one think of anything else, how could one live any other adventure?" But Habonim would not provide transportation to Palestine for a sixteen-year-old. With a survivor's impunity, Friedländer altered his birth certificate to make himself two years older. Then he joined Betar, the Irgun youth movement that was pledged to fight for "the whole of the historic homeland" of the Jewish people, east and west of the Jordan River.

BROTHERS AT WAR

Early in June 1948, Friedländer received instructions to report to the Gare de Lyon station for a train to Marseilles. To leave for Israel, he realized, meant "joining my fate to a common lot, and also a dream of communion and community." The night before his departure for Israel he wrote to his godparents: ". . . recent events have awakened a feeling in my soul that had been dormant for a long time, the feeling that I was Jewish. And I want to prove it by leaving to fight alongside all the Jews who are dying in Palestine. . . ."

With the arrival of the caravan of French army trucks in Port-du-Bouc, port workers were dismissed. Only Irgun officials and French authorities were permitted to enter a closed zone surrounding the dock, where French soldiers unloaded and stacked crates of weapons until 2 a.m. Several hours later, after stevedores had reported for work, a mishandled crate dropped from a loading crane, whether by accident or design, breaking open and spilling rifles across the pier. The longshoremen, many of whom were Arabs, refused to continue loading. Their hasty departure left French soldiers and *Altalena* passengers to complete the job, working all day and through the next night. The arsenal included 300 Bren guns, 50 German Spender guns, 500 anti-tank guns, 1000 grenades and 5 million rounds of ammunition.

Members of the Irgun command in France — Lankin, Stavsky and Ben-Ami — boarded early to prepare for departure. In Israel, however, Begin was reluctant to violate both the June agreement with Galili prohibiting the arrival of weapons and the impending United Nations cease-fire. He told his colleagues: "We may not take upon ourselves responsibility for the possible consequences of its breach." But after their prolonged efforts to secure financing for the *Altalena*, and extended negotiations with the French government, the Irgun disapora leadership in France was determined to sail.

At sunrise on June 11, trucks transported nine hundred and forty passengers — including 120 young women — from the Irgun training camp outside Marseilles. When a group arrived with musical instruments — "a dilapidated accordion, violin and mandolin" — it became, Warshaw recalled, "a Jewish fiesta." They boarded in groups organized by their fifteen countries of origin. A small cohort of young men from Cuba formed the last contingent. There was space on board for triple the number of passengers, but Haganah representatives had declined an invitation to allow immigrants identified with their movement to sail on the Irgun ship. Just before departure, Fein subsequently reported, "a messenger returned from Palestine" with communication procedures and landing instructions. He understood this to mean that the arrival of the *Altalena* "had been completely agreed to and approved by the government" of Israel.

The *Altalena* crew, like its passengers, was a heterogeneous mix, with Americans (all but two of whom were Jews) in the majority. Captain Fein, radio operator Leslie Solomon, 1st mate Jack Baron, the 1st engineer, the electrician and two of the able-bodied seamen came from the United States. Others arrived from France, Germany, Poland, Lithuania, Canada and Israel. The chief cook was French; his assistant came from Manhattan's Lower East Side. A doctor who had been active in the French underground and intended to practice medicine in Israel volunteered to serve as the ship's physician. Julian Berenson, an American Navy veteran, volunteered because he "wanted to do [his] share in the fight for Jewish freedom." London-born Nathan Cashman, who had never belonged to a Zionist organization, impulsively decided that he would leave England "and look for a boat going to Palestine." In Marseilles he talked his way on board the *Altalena*; despite his absence of maritime experience he was designated a seaman.

At twilight on June 11th, just before the beginning of the Jewish Sabbath and the United Nations ceasefire, the *Altalena* pulled away from the same port where the *Exodus* had departed eleven months earlier. There was a "rhythmical shuddering of the deck," Friedländer long remembered. Mark Hasten, a veteran of the Polish Brigade of the Soviet army during World War II, felt "a sense of Jewish pride" and "subdued, yet heartfelt, excitement." He noticed a small boat, flying the Israeli flag, following alongside the *Altalena* as it left the harbor. From its deck Eli Tavin, the Irgun overseas intelligence chief, waved enthusiastically.

Nearly a thousand people on board sang *Hatikvah*. "We had been the dregs — the humiliated victims of Europe's greatest bloodbath," Hasten realized, "but now we were soldiers on an age-old quest to free our beloved homeland." Itik Gikenitsky, one of many Holocaust survivors aboard, remembered the moment: "We had been persecuted and humiliated. . . . Suddenly, you're a soldier. You're armed, rushing to fight for your homeland. . . . This was our greatest dream."

At midnight Irgun leaders on board heard a BBC broadcast that Israel and warring Arab states had accepted the United Nations ceasefire. Under its terms, the importation of arms and men of military age was prohibited for one month. The BBC also reported that an Irgun ship, transporting weapons and hundreds of fighting men, had sailed from Port-du-Bouc. The American Consul in Marseilles sent an "Urgent" cable to the State Department reporting the departure of a "Jewish immigrant ship" for Palestine with "800 Jewish volunteers and a shipment of arms."

The BBC broadcast caught Irgun leaders on board by surprise. "We had not expected this international announcement of our secret mission," Lankin wrote. "Now with the world apprised of our movements, the probability of an attack stared us brutally in the face." But no one on board imagined that the attack would come from the government of the State of Israel.

After heading south, along the west coast of Italy toward Sicily, the *Altalena* turned east. On the "flat calm" Mediterranean, Captain Fein navigated a zig-zag course to avoid detection. The ship traveled mostly by night, taking eleven days for a five-day journey. Irgun leaders tried, without success, to make radio contact with command headquarters in Israel and its broadcasting station in France for updated instructions. Contingency plans were quickly developed for the ship to remain at sea, if necessary, for the duration of the truce.

In Tel Aviv Menachem Begin, hearing a repeat of the BBC broadcast, decided to stop the ship, at least temporarily, while the truce remained in force. His aide Zipporah Levy repeatedly radioed his orders to the *Altalena*: "Keep away — await instructions." Begin, she remembered, "was very calm but determined to stop them." But no one aboard the *Altalena*, cut off by faulty radio connections from their command in Israel and staff in Paris, could hear the urgent message.

Disregarding the potential hazards of the mission, Irgun leaders on board were determined to complete it. "We regarded the war in Israel as a life-and-death struggle," Lankin wrote, and the military supplies on the *Altalena* "could change the course of the war." In anticipation of a British naval attack on the ship, Bren machine guns were mounted on deck. American and British soldiers with World War II experience, led by a commando who had served in France and a former marine who had fought in the Pacific, underwent rigorous daily training to form the nucleus of a special fighting unit should there be an emergency landing in "hostile territory." With the possibility of an extended journey to wait out the truce, food and water were carefully rationed.

Despite the potential dangers and precautionary measures, passengers shared a sense of anticipation and exultation. "Train by day," one recalled, "We would sing all night." After so many years of suffering and wandering, "people found each other." Young Friedländer, like many of his companions, was "struck with wonder by the sea, our heads full of our dreams." Hebrew language instruction was provided; lectures were given. But there was hard work to be done, removing guns from their crates and coating them with grease to protect them from dampness. Friedländer spent long hours below deck, preparing cartridge belts for machine-guns. On the second afternoon Captain Fein performed a wedding ceremony on deck; the *ketuba* (marriage contract) had been prepared on the ship's typewriter. Passengers celebrated with joyous dancing, accompanied by accordions, guitars, harmonicas, balalaikas and violins — and wine from the galley.

That night, after the celebration ended, Fein, Stavsky and Lankin gathered in the radio room to resume attempts to contact their commanders in Israel. "We had almost given up when, through the static, we heard a young woman's voice calling our code names." It was Begin's personal secretary, Yael, repeating a message in English: "Listen to me: Keep away! Keep away!" But no further radio contact was possible. Begin wired Irgun headquarters in Paris: "She can't come home now." But to Lankin, the Irgun commander on board, "it was almost unbearable to contemplate the thought of the *Altalena*'s precious cargo never reaching the shores of Israel. I told Fein to continue en route to Israel with all possible speed."

Even before leaving Port-du-Bouc the *Altalena* had been closely monitored by Israeli intelligence operatives. They knew the contents of its cargo, its departure date and its destination in Israel. Nonetheless, news of its leaving aroused mounting suspicion in government and military circles. Isar Harel, director of the Haganah intelligence service that carefully monitored its journey, suspected that its weapons would be used for Irgun purposes contrary to government policy. Palmach Colonel Meir Pa'il was dismayed that although the government itself was continuing to import weapons covertly in violation of the cease-fire, the Irgun was engaging in a flamboyant public display of disobedience.

On June 15th, Begin met once again with Deputy Defense Minister Galili to update the government on the *Altalena*. The purpose of the meeting, according to Begin, was to provide representatives of the Defense Ministry with "all the information about the *Altalena* and to request the government's decision as to whether the ship should or should not arrive during the ceasefire." An aide presented "the details about the *Altalena*, its people and equipment." Begin remained willing "that the government decide and tell us whether the *Altalena* should proceed and arrive in Israel, or whether we should send it back." His proposal that its weapons and munitions be stored in Irgun warehouses, under joint supervision with the IDF, was rejected. Galili promised to respond further after consultation with his superiors — meaning, of course, Ben-Gurion.

The next morning, Galili telephoned Begin: "We agree to the arrival of the vessel. As quickly as possible." To avoid UN aerial surveillance the ship was instructed to land at Kfar Vitkin, a moshav near Netanya, some twenty miles north of Tel Aviv. Lankin was delighted with the news. Kfar Vitkin, after all, was a Haganah stronghold: "If Begin was ordering us to anchor at Kfar Vitkin — the lion's den of the Irgun's political adversaries in Israel — then an agreement must have been negotiated between us." It was, for Lankin, "a clear sign of cooperation in the *Altalena*'s landing — a sign of internal harmony, of brotherhood." For Begin, "worry was replaced by joy."

On June 16th, Ben-Gurion mentioned the *Altalena* in his diary for the first time: "Tomorrow or the next day their ship is due to arrive." He noted, in detail, its military contents, concluding: "They should not be turned back. They should be sent to an unknown beach." The government plan, Haganah intelligence chief Harel recalled, was to equip Irgun units to fight anywhere beyond Israeli rule. That, of course, meant Jerusalem.

But there remained an ominously unresolved problem: the distribution of weapons and munitions. Ben-Gurion understood the June 3rd meeting to have assured agreement that the Irgun would place "all its weapons and military equipment at the disposal of the High Command of the Israel Defense Forces." But Begin, consistent with his own understanding of the agreement, had continued to insist that twenty percent of the weapons would be allocated for the Irgun fighting forces in Jerusalem. He wanted the remainder to go to Irgun units in the Israel Defense Forces or be stored in their own armories.

Galili, according to Shmuel Katz, a member of the Irgun High Command, "indicated that the request for Jerusalem would be considered favorably." (According to Ben-Gurion's diary, however, "Yisrael [Galili] told me that IZL, contrary to his instructions, decided to send weapons to Jerusalem.") Galili did not agree that the remaining eighty percent of the weapons would be distributed directly to Irgun battalions in the IDF. According to their understanding, Galili insisted, the Irgun must turn over all military equipment and weapons to the Israel Defense Forces "without any conditions."

There was disagreement among Begin's advisers, some of whom — especially Hillel Kook — rejected any precedent for distributing weapons in the army according to political quotas. After the group reached consensus, Begin telephoned Galili to report their revised position: "We insist on one condition only — 20% of the arms should go to the Irgun in Jerusalem. The rest goes to the I.D.F. units according to general staff decisions." Galili agreed, but rejected Begin's insistence that the remainder go solely to Irgun units in the Israel Defense Forces.

Under pressure from Katz, who opposed discrimination either for or against the Irgun, Begin again telephoned Galili and agreed that the remainder would go to the army. No agreement was reached as to where the arms would be stored and under whose control. But Galili advised Ben-Gurion that "a new and dangerous situation has arisen: a demand for a kind of private army, with private weapons, for certain units in the army." Ben-Gurion was fiercely determined that Zionist factionalism must yield to a unitary government and military under his exclusive command. He would not tolerate the existence of "private armies" — neither the Irgun on the right nor, six months later, the Palmach on the left.

Within the nascent Jewish state a fierce struggle was simmering over political, no less than geographical, boundaries. For fifteen years, ever since the Arlosoroff murder, left and right had clashed over the meaning and future of Zionism. After barely one month of national sovereignty, their struggle would reach its tragic climax on the beaches of Kfar Vitkin and Tel Aviv.

Shortly before sunset on June 19th, *Altalena* passengers and crew caught their first glimpse of the coast of Israel. "Our Zionist volunteers from all over the world," Lankin remembered, "soldiers, exiles, concentration camp survivors, people who had lost so much and had so much to gain — all clung to the deck railings and strained their eyes.... We had reached the Promised Land." Nearing shore in darkness, a small boat was dispatched to make contact with

Irgun representatives and coordinate plans for landing and unloading.

But the *Altalena* had mistakenly arrived at a power station at the edge of Tel Aviv, more than twenty miles south of its destination. After a brief flurry of gunfire with local Israeli coastguardsmen on duty, who had mistaken them for hostile attackers, the Irgun men were permitted to return to the ship, which sailed up the coast searching for the twin red signal lights that marked its destination. After midnight it finally arrived at the Kfar Vitkin beach, but high waves prevented a landing. The ship was instructed to pull back out to sea and return the next evening.

That night Ben-Gurion called the Cabinet into an emergency session. There were reports that Irgun soldiers were leaving their IDF units to assist in the unloading of weapons on the beach. Foreign Minister Moshe Shertok warned the ministers: "We may now be facing a blatant, public violation of the truce by Jews, without our being personally responsible for it. I am speaking here of an Etzel [Irgun] operation." Ben-Gurion restated the June 3rd agreement under which the Irgun had promised "to put all its weapons and military equipment at the disposal of the High Command of the Israel Defense Forces" and "cease operations within the State of Israel and all areas under the jurisdiction of the Government of Israel."

Ben-Gurion was adamant: "There are not going to be two armies. And Mr. Begin will not do whatever he feels like. We must decide whether to hand over power to Begin or tell him to cease his separatist activities. If he does not give in, we shall open fire." The Cabinet unanimously agreed: "The Government charges the Defense Minister with taking action in accordance with the laws of the land." Ben-Gurion noted: "Taking action means shooting."

After sailing west for eight hours the *Altalena* turned back toward Israel. "It was a beautiful sight to see the coast of Eretz closing in on us," a passenger recalled. Viewing the shoreline, Yitzhaq Ben-Ami had sudden flashbacks to his Tel Aviv childhood, his military training by the Yarkon River, and the cemetery where his parents were buried. He felt a burst of pride: "We were coming home to a free country." During the aborted landing the night before, Captain Fein had discovered that an underwater shelf prevented the ship from reaching shore. He halted the *Altalena* forty meters from the end of a small pier extending from the beach. It was 9 p.m. on Sunday, June 20.

Menachem Begin came by motorboat from shore to greet the new arrivals, who responded with "an ear-splitting cheer." They "milled around him, drunk with excitement." Irgun fighters "touched him, they shook his hand, they called out thank you, congratulations and endearments." Landing the *Altalena*, wrote Shmuel Katz, "seemed a fitting last act" for the Irgun. For Begin, "it was a great and historic occasion," symbolically ending his long struggle as an underground renegade.

Within two hours, as Irgun fighters departed in units, nearly all the passengers had disembarked. From the beach they were transported to a camp in nearby Netanya where they could rest briefly before their induction into the army. Then the arduous task of unloading cargo began. Several dozen men remained behind to bring the crates of weapons to shore in a launch, two lifeboats, and small craft provided by local volunteers. They did so, Lankin observed, "with a kind of fanatical ecstasy." Two young women grabbed a heavy box of ammunition and ran with it "as if it were a box of chocolates." Some Palmach men arrived, ostensibly to help, but after boarding and inspecting the ship they departed and were not seen again. On the beach, "khaki-clad men ran about shouting orders; groups marched in all directions; motors revved up."

But amid the euphoria there were ominous signs. Earlier that night Captain Fein had noticed "two unidentified ships" a mile offshore, identified at daybreak as Israeli navy corvettes. Israeli naval commander Paul Shulman (a United States Navy veteran and *Exodus* deckhand) ordered the corvettes to approach the *Altalena* and monitor the debarkation and unloading, which proceeded "slowly and in a disorderly manner." He observed "about a hundred armed IZL men" on the beach, "but not at the ready. . . . They were not arranged for defense. They worked slowly, not in a hurry or *schvitz* [sweat]." The Irgun men, Shulman noted, "nicely welcomed the people in our boat."

Reports filtered in that Irgun soldiers who had left their IDF units to help with the unloading had been stopped and detained on the road from Netanya. Israeli soldiers under the command of Moshe Dayan had begun to surround the debarkation area. Begin's chief of operations, Amihai Paglin, advised him to return the weapons to the ship, which should pull back to sea until the truce ended. Begin would not consider the suggestion. He seemed unruffled, assuring Lankin that "an arrangement" with the government was imminent.

In a meeting attended by Chief of Operations Yadin, army officers were briefed by Galili. According to Dan Even, commander of the Alexandroni Brigade on the beach at Kfar Vitkin, Galili reported the impending arrival of "a boat filled with arms and ammunition." Galili acknowledged: "We knew the arms were due to arrive and reached an agreement whereby we and they were to unload the arms together." But after Galili's briefing, and with Yadin's authorization, Even prepared for the possibility of military action.

Yadin assured Cabinet ministers that there were sufficient military personnel — six hundred IDF soldiers already at Kfar Vitkin, with reinforcements available from two battalions — "if it proved necessary to use force." He asked bluntly: "What are our orders?" Foreign Minister Shertok proposed that five hundred men be sent to Kfar Vitkin "to break up the Etzel concentration, as well as to disarm and arrest all the people coming off the boat." Ben-Gurion indicated that he was "ready to act in accordance with the law, if he had enough forces at his disposal to do so." He added: "To act meant to shoot, . . . a very grave matter indeed." Rabbi Fishman warned that a battle would endanger both sides; perhaps the threat of force would suffice. Ben-Gurion responded: "A threat is meaningful only if it is backed up by a willingness to carry it out."

BROTHERS AT WAR

The next morning the Government Press Office announced: "The Government regards this attempt by an independent group to bring in arms, particularly during the truce period, as a grave violation of Israel's laws and of her international obligations, as well as an infringement of the clear agreement reached recently with the heads of Etzel . . . [who] were to accept the authority of the State." The government and military command "are determined to stamp out immediately this traitorous attempt to deny the authority of the State of Israel and of its representatives."

When last-minute attempts to reach agreement failed, Galili drafted an ultimatum for Commander Even to deliver to Begin. It ordered "confiscation of all weapons and war materials," to be turned over to the State of Israel and placed with Even for safekeeping. Shortly before noon on June 21st, Even delivered the message to Irgun leaders on the Kfar Vitkin beach. If military supplies were not relinquished, he warned, "I will immediately use all the means at my disposal to implement the order. . . . You have ten minutes in which to reply." The purpose of the operation, Even instructed his officers, "is to force the Irgun to turn over to the Army the weapons that arrived on the LST." Ben-Gurion demanded: "Either they accept orders and carry them out, or [we] shoot." Rejecting further negotiations, he insisted: "The time for agreements has passed . . . [and] force must be applied without hesitation." In his own handwriting, Ben-Gurion added: "*Immediately.*"

On board the *Altalena*, Lankin was "stunned" by the ultimatum. Begin tried to reassure him that Meridor would meet with Even to reach an understanding to prevent bloodshed. A United Nations plane flew low overhead; the Israeli navy corvettes moved into position to block passage to the west; word arrived that Israeli soldiers had surrounded the beachhead. On shore Dov Shilansky, who had disembarked from the *Altalena*, encountered an Israeli soldier in a command car. "I spoke to him in Hebrew," he recalled. "It was my first speech in Israel." Shilansky (who would become Speaker of the Knesset in 1988) told him: "We've just arrived. We survived the Holocaust. We've come here to fight by your side. The

CIVIL WAR?

homeland is in danger. We will join the army." He was instructed to go no further. Shilansky replied: "We have no other way. I won't go back to Dachau. If we can't come to Israel, we'll go back to the sea." The soldier replied: "I don't care. Go back to the sea." By then Kfar Vitkin had been completely sealed off by Commander Even's soldiers.

At a nearby military airport orders were received to prepare several planes for a possible bombing run over the *Altalena*. One of the pilots, Boris Senior, had served in the British Royal Air Force during World War II. After the war ended and he learned about the Holocaust, he joined the Irgun, immigrated to Palestine, and enlisted in the air force. Ordered to take off and bomb the *Altalena*, he angrily refused: "I will never be capable of bombing my Jewish brethren." When other pilots also decided not to participate, the mission was aborted.

Late that afternoon, Begin summoned several dozen Irgun men on the beach into formation to apprise them of negotiations with the IDF. He walked inside their open rectangle and began to speak. Suddenly Israeli soldiers raked the beach with machine-gun bullets and mortar shells. Within moments, Yitzhaq Ben-Ami recalled, "we were in a state of uncontrolled siege." Yaacov Meridor, Begin's second in command, ordered: "Don't shoot back." An Irgun fighter realized: "I couldn't shoot. My brother was on the other side." "We were confused and ashamed at the same time," another remembered, "instead of welcoming us they were killing and wounding many of our men whose only purpose was to help."

With darkness falling, Ben-Ami and a friend from their Betar days took refuge in a sandy foxhole. Ben-Ami asked him if he had read Josephus. "Do you remember the description of the final days in the defense of Jerusalem . . . [when] the Judeans continued to massacre each other. . . . Doesn't this look like the Third destruction of the Temple?" Ben-Ami recalled: "Thus I spent my first night on the soil of free Israel, dodging the bullets of my brothers."

In the wheelhouse of the *Altalena*, Julian Berenson, the 43-year-old American navy veteran, lifted his rifle "to shoot . . . those who were shooting at us. But then I thought: Who am I, going to shoot and kill Jews! And I put my rifle down." Some IDF soldiers refused to obey orders. Yeshayahu Yarimi protested: "I'm here to fight the enemy. I won't fight another Jew." He instructed the soldiers in his squad: "Do what your conscience tells you." Yarimi was one of eight soldiers to be court-martialed for their disobedience that day. Six Irgun men and two IDF soldiers died in the fighting at Kfar Vitkin. The years of animosity between Zionist political enemies had finally, and catastrophically, exploded in violence.

As chaos erupted on the beach, Captain Fein suspected "a sneak Arab attack." He restarted the engines, intending to head out to sea to protect the ship. But the Irgun high command — Begin, Stavsky, Lankin, and Merlin — had decided to board the *Altalena* and sail south to Tel Aviv. Begin wanted an opportunity to communicate directly with the government and, according to Shmuel Katz, "put an end to what [he] still hoped was a perilous misunderstanding somewhere." The Irgun could also expect stronger public support in Tel Aviv than Kfar Vitkin. ("Whatever plots were brewing in Ben-Gurion's mind," Ben-Ami wrote, "could not be carried out in Tel-Aviv, in full view of thousands of people.") When the launch carrying the Irgun leaders came under machine-gun fire from the navy corvettes Fein maneuvered the *Altalena* to provide a shield, enabling them to board safely.

Commander Even informed the government that the Irgun had surrendered and agreed to turn over all weapons on shore to the IDF. Under army supervision, armored vehicles left the beach packed with English rifles, Bren guns and ammunition. An Israeli army communique reported that the Kfar Vitkin beach had been "seized by the dissidents" (who, in fact, had been instructed by the government to land there). As an IDF army unit approached them, "the Irgun opened fire using machine-guns, anti-tank weapons and one mortar" (an "attack" uncorroborated by any other source). The army's objective had been "to force unconditional surrender" and compel the Irgun to relinquish weapons and vehicles and abide by military orders. Ben-Gurion wrote in his diary: "IZL Day. What was destined to happen — finally happened." He enumerated the military supplies that were seized at Kfar Vitkin: 2,080,000 English cartridges, 1473 English rifles, 30 to 40 Bren guns, 5 English piats, 3300 English piat shells, and 60 boxes filled with other weapons. The crisis seemed to have abated.

Trailed down the coast by the navy vessels, there were intermittent gunfire exchanges as the *Altalena* maneuvered to prevent another ship from slipping between it and the shore. Shortly after midnight on June 21 the *Altalena* ran aground, 150 meters off the Tel Aviv beach at the end of Frishman Street, opposite Palmach headquarters in the Ritz Hotel. Captain Fein remembered: "We hit the beach at top speed and settled down to await daylight and further developments."

There was a flurry of attempts to resolve the crisis without renewed violence. Several local village mayors approached Ben-Gurion, who spent the night at army headquarters in Ramat Gan outside Tel Aviv, to demand a ceasefire. Unknown to the Prime Minister, Interior Minister Gruenbaum had met with Avraham Stavsky to discuss the distribution of weapons from the *Altalena*. Gruenbaum's independent action infuriated other ministers. "The main question here," Shertok had insisted at the Cabinet meeting the day before, "is the sovereignty of the State of Israel.... We must use every means at our disposal, including military force, to make Etzel accept Government policy." To Labor Minister Mordechai Bentov there was "no alternative: either the Government acts as a government should, or it will be clear to the entire world that it is helpless. We cannot retreat."

Ben-Gurion reiterated: "The State's authority is the main principle." The lines were clearly drawn, he insisted: "There can be no State without an army under the control of the Government." The arrival of the *Altalena* off the Tel Aviv shore, and reports received by Deputy Chief of Staff Zvi Ayalon that Irgun soldiers who had abandoned their posts were arriving in Tel Aviv with "plans to attack IDF headquarters," stoked fears of an insurrection.

BROTHERS AT WAR

Thirty minutes after the *Altalena* beached off shore, Yigael Yadin conferred with Galili before reporting to Ben-Gurion. Hearing his report, Ben-Gurion decided that force was inevitable. At an urgent 4 a.m. meeting, Chief of Naval Operations Shmuel Yanai assured Ben-Gurion that the *Altalena* could be disabled without gunfire by using smoke grenades and boarding the ship from nearby navy vessels. But the Prime Minister, Yanai recalled, was "pacing nervously from side to side, talking and yelling." He was "upset and angry. ... He shouted at everyone." Yanai concluded: "His aim was ... to destroy the munitions on the *Altalena*" as the only way to prevent civil war. Ben-Gurion demanded that "the ship be turned over to the Government immediately, and if necessary use force to back up that demand."

Unwilling to negotiate further with the Irgun, Ben-Gurion insisted upon forcing "the enemy . . . to unconditional surrender, by all the means and methods available." After considering various alternatives — including permitting the *Altalena* to sail peacefully away — the Cabinet decided, by a 7-2 vote, "to demand that the ship be turned over to the State."

Ben-Gurion ordered Commander Yadin to act in accordance with the Cabinet decision. The General Staff issued orders, signed by Yadin, to the Kiryati Brigade, the Artillery Corps, the Navy, and Air Force, "to bring the enemy on the ship docked at Tel Aviv harbor to surrender by all means at our disposal. . . . Be ready for the beginning of the operation and opening of fire, according to my order and in line with the instructions of the government of Israel." There would be "warning fire"; then a demand for "unconditional surrender"; finally, if necessary, "a continued operation until it reaches a conclusion."

At a press conference, Foreign Minister Shertok announced: "The Government is resolved to maintain its sovereignty and its ability to fulfill its international obligations. It will not permit undisciplined armed groups to foster political and military anarchy. The Etzel ship must be turned over to the Government immediately and unconditionally." Nothing, he insisted, was more important than "upholding State authority." Galili, who had represented the government in negotiations with Begin since mid-May, added (erroneously): "the I.Z.L. has broken the agreement. They did not inform us of the date of the boat's arrival nor where it was going to anchor." With the State "engaged in civil war," he asserted, the government had "no choice but to resort to force."

But there were problems with the government plan. Just as pilots had refused to bomb the *Altalena* at Kfar Vitkin, Haganah commander Michael Ben-Gal expressed doubts that he could "rouse his men to the action" ordered by the government. The High Command turned instead to the Palmach, certain that its "ideological animus toward the dissenters" would overcome any constraints. Yigal Allon, the Palmach commander who had played a significant role in combating the Irgun during the Season, was instructed by the General Staff to launch operation "Purge" against IZL "forces" — comprising several dozen men still on board the *Altalena*.

Ben-Gurion told him, Allon recounted, "Yigal, we are facing an open rebellion. . . . The entire future of this country is in the balance." In a dramatic tone, he demanded: "Get Begin!" Yadin added: "You might have to kill Jews." Allon suggested that a cannon be deployed to threaten shelling; if the Irgun did not surrender, it would be fired. Yadin and Ben-Gurion agreed. Allon was convinced (according to biographer Anita Shapira) "that he was fighting against the forces of fascism threatening to take over the state." The Kiryati brigade was supplied with a battery of 65-mm cannons.

At 8:30 that morning a 26-year-old Palmach officer, Yitzhak Rabin, arrived at Palmach headquarters at the Ritz Hotel. He was looking for his girl friend Leah, who worked for the information department. Informed by Allon that Irgun men from the *Altalena* were "trying to take control of the beach and unload the arms," Rabin was appointed commander of the Palmach headquarters building, where battalion police were stationed among convalescing soldiers. "Rumor follows rumor," he remembered: "The IZL wants to take over all of Tel Aviv . . . no, even that is not enough . . . it intends to forcibly take control of the new state." Outside Palmach headquarters, "confusion reigns. No one knew what to expect." Windows and doors were sandbagged.

In mid-morning, a launch was lowered from the ship carrying a dozen men, 30 rifles, 6 submachine guns and one anti-tank bazooka. From the bridge of the *Altalena* Joe Kohn observed "truck-loads of soldiers taking up positions on houses and high ground above the beach." As the launch approached shore, two machine-gun crews were ordered to fire; they refused. Their commander, Moshe Keren, was ordered to shoot at his insubordinate soldiers. He replied: "Not that." His superior officer arrived to command the crews to open fire; again they refused. Elsewhere on the beach flurries of gunfire targeted the new Irgun arrivals. The launch, quickly unloaded by Irgun men on shore, returned to the ship.

After a piat shell exploded below Palmach headquarters (Rabin recalled in a 1983 interview), "we arrive[d] at the conclusion that there is no choice but to wipe them out from our midst. . . ." Rabin and another officer went to the roof and threw grenades at "the separatist forces" on the beach. (Some fighters had gathered for protection at an adjacent building, where Palmach and Irgun soldiers amicably shared cold drinks.) Rabin remembered: "Irgun people got hurt. One of their units raised a white flag. They requested a pause to evacuate the wounded. We called for ambulances." While the battle raged, hundreds of Israelis gathered near the beach to watch Jews attacking Jews.

When the launch left the *Altalena* at 11:30 to return to shore, "all hell broke loose." Bursts of gunfire from IDF positions on the beach, and from overlooking buildings, strafed the shore and the ship. "We were suddenly in the midst of war," Lankin realized, "yet it was not Arabs or British firing upon us, spilling our blood, but our fellow Jews." Two *Altalena* crew members were killed and Irgun leader Avraham Stavsky was mortally wounded. He died, Eri Jabotinsky wrote bitterly, on the same beach where Arlosoroff was murdered — "and at the hands of the same man, Ben-Gurion, who had unsuccessfully tried to hang him then."

CIVIL WAR?

To Arbel Zerubavel, Yigal Allon's intelligence officer, it was clearly "a rebellion against the State of Israel," requiring that the "dissidents" be "wiped out." Zerubavel had "no hesitation" about firing, nor did he have "even a shadow of regret." Allon, he remembered, acted without "any hesitation about *milchemet achim* [war of brothers]." But Palmach soldier Amnon Dror recalled: "Firing on each other: it seemed illogical, unbelievable. I had many doubts, when I pointed the gun at the approaching boat filled with Jews." But he overcame them: "You tell yourself, you are guarding Israeli democracy. And with this belief, you shoot."

But some soldiers in the Kiryati Brigade, "unable to face the difficult necessity to prevent the acts of the IZL," left their weapons behind and departed fom the beach. In a regiment of foreign volunteers (Mahal), David Migdal witnessed "Jews killing other Jews" and refused to participate. Given the choice by their commander to obey orders or go to jail, Mahal soldiers carried their weapons but emptied them of ammunition. Irgun member Abba Groznick remembered: "If Begin had told us to fight we would have, but he did not want war between brothers and we accepted his leadership." Irgun fighters did not return fire.

Shortly after noon, the government convened an emergency meeting to deal with the crisis. Ben-Gurion was sharply attacked by right-wing and religious party members, led by Interior Minister Gruenbaum. He accused Galili of reporting falsely and Ben-Gurion of obstructing efforts to end the crisis without violence. Gruenbaum insisted: "We must negotiate. . . the 800 immigrants who came on the ship have already been removed and dispersed." But Agriculture Minister Aharon Zizling responded: "We are facing an open rebellion. . . . A political coup is being deliberately aimed against the army command." Ben-Gurion warned: "This is an attempt to destroy the army. This is an attempt to kill the state." There would be "no negotiations — but only surrender of the ship to the Government and acceptance of all army orders." By a 7-2 vote, the Irgun was instructed to surrender the *Altalena*.

BROTHERS AT WAR

On the beach Rabin managed to reach an agreement with Irgun fighters to stop the shooting before it provoked "a mutual massacre." An Irgun officer, he remembered, shouted: "Why are you shooting at Jews? Why at Jews?" Rabin replied: "When Jews stop shooting at us, we will stop shooting at Jews." Government representative David Cohen, standing in water up to his knees, broadcast by loudspeaker to the *Altalena*: "A representative of the Government and the army will board the ship and arrange to have the people taken off, help the wounded and unloading of cargo." In reply, from the *Altalena* loudspeaker, came the message: "We want to negotiate. . . . We don't want to have war with our brothers." Urgent pleas were repeated for a boat to remove the wounded and dying. It was promised, but never arrived. Negotiations foundered over the government demand for an unconditional Irgun surrender and relinquishment of all weapons to the IDF. But by early afternoon a tenuous cease-fire was in place.

At 4 p.m., Ben-Gurion ordered Yadin (who subsequently claimed that he only intended "warning shots") to resume firing. "All of a sudden," recalled a Haganah soldier, "we heard a shot from the north. . . . It was a cannon." The crew commander, Hilary Dilesky, was a volunteer from South Africa who had arrived in Israel only two months earlier. There were four cannons in his battery; his was chosen to fire the first shot. Receiving his orders, he recalled, "I suddenly was struck with a heavy, deep feeling that I didn't want to shoot."

Dilesky approached a group of high-ranking officers to speak to his corps commander. He said — in English, for he could not yet speak Hebrew: "I hadn't come to Israel to fight Jews." The commander yelled back that his job was to obey orders. It was, Dilesky recalled nearly fifty years later, "a fateful moment" when he realized that "following orders was the right thing to do." But "my heart was broken when we began firing," he confessed. "This has been a burden all my life, and still is."

In rapid succession, three cannon shells passed near the *Altalena*, exploding harmlessly in the sea. Captain Fein conferred with Begin, advising him that with a direct hit, "the ship, the cargo and possibly a good many lives would be lost." Before Begin could renew radio contact with Irgun headquarters on shore, the cannon fire resumed. Fein ordered the Star of David lowered and raised a white flag of surrender. Moments later, a cannon shell slammed into the *Altalena*, igniting a blazing fire in the cargo hold. Crewmen raced below to open the hose valves but they were unable to extinguish it. "Smoke billowed from all the portholes and ventilators," Lankin remembered; "the deck was enveloped in a thick black pall." Fein ordered everyone to abandon ship.

Dr. Shalom Weiss, a navy doctor on board the nearby *Wedgwood*, saw the white flag waving from the *Altalena*. But shooting from the beach continued: "Rifle and machine-gun fire kept hitting living targets." On the navy ship *Eilat*, crewmember Eli Warshavsky remembered "escaping men shot in the water." From the beach Azriel Carlebach, editor of the daily newspaper *Ma'ariv*, witnessed "Jewish young men . . . with steel helmets on their heads and machine guns in their hand, ready to fire. . . . In the sea, on the mast of the ship, and on its deck, Jews stand, waving a white flag, and shouting: 'Don't fire!'" But as men jumped overboard, Joe Kohn observed from the bridge that "continuous small arms fire from shore . . . was directed at everyone in the water." A 17-year-old Haganah soldier never forgot that "there were people on our side who waited until they saw heads above water, and then they fired at them."

Uri Yarom, a young Palmach soldier (who would command Israel's first helicopter squadron) was stunned by what he witnessed: "The wounded were being lowered off the boat. From the shore people started swimming toward them to offer help, but from the hotel and nearby houses indiscriminate shots were aimed at the helpless wounded and those who swam to rescue them!" He long remembered the fighter wearing a *Hashomer Hatzair* (Socialist Zionist) uniform "who directed the snipers to their targets and pointed to each head that bobbed above the water's surface. . . . Before my eyes was waged a war between brothers. Jews are shooting Jews — in order to kill!" A French volunteer swimming ashore was hit by gunfire and drowned. Israel Gorelnik, a 20-year-old Palmach soldier, was assigned the "very difficult" task of guarding Irgun fighters who arrived amid the gunfire. They asked him: "What are you doing to us?"

It was chaotic and traumatic: "screams in the water pierced the air, bullets were spraying the decks and whistling everywhere." Irgun men on the beach, Rabin recalled, were in "total hysteria," shouting "Begin is on the ship." Palmach soldiers, excited by the prospect of finally eliminating their political nemesis, opened fire "as if from a feeling of wanting to kill Begin." The Irgun leader remained on board, supervising the lowering of the wounded, including the dying Stavsky, into small kayaks that were frantically rowed out from shore. Begin was among the last to leave, followed by Lankin and Fein who jumped into the sea just before a series of violent explosions engulfed the *Altalena* in flames. "In the final salvo," Lankin wrote, "millions of bullets from the crates exploded, a dream gone up in smoke and fire."

That day in Tel Aviv, ten men from the *Altalena* and one IDF soldier were killed in the fighting. It was, Rabin remembered, "a terrible day, a black day." But he remained convinced that Ben-Gurion had made the "brave decision to forcibly put an end to a situation of two Jewish armies where one decides to provide itself with weapons."

Once safely ashore, Lankin and Fein were taken to Irgun headquarters, where distraught spokesmen tried to answer questions from a swarm of journalists. Later that evening, Lankin's sister-in-law arrived to bring them to her home. There, seeking "respite from the nightmare," the captain and the commander fell into exhausted sleep. But not for long: soldiers armed with submachine guns surrounded the building and an army officer arrived to supervise their removal to a nearby military camp. "Dead tired and depressed," they were interrogated and placed under guard.

Lankin subsequently reflected: "Perhaps this was naïve on our part. We truly believed that the political differences between us would be ironed out later. . . . I felt deeply ashamed that while fighting for its very life against the Arabs, Israel still could not make peace within its own family." Fein, interviewed several days later by an Associated Press reporter, stated: "the Government knew the ship was coming. . . . It was the Government who designated Kfar Vitkin as the place on the coast where we were to land and unload."

Tel Aviv, a city in turmoil, was placed under curfew. While soldiers fired from the beach Irgun sympathizers drove through the streets with loudspeakers, imploring supporters to witness the attack on the *Altalena*. Moshe Lovy and a group of Betar friends from nearby Ramat Gan drove into Tel Aviv along back roads to avoid military blockades. Entering the city, they encountered Haganah soldiers on patrol, armed with machine guns. Heading to Frishman Street they were halted by a Sherman tank, whose crew commanded them to proceed to a former British military camp nearby, where they were questioned about their political affiliations and confined for two days. Recounting the episode, Lovy suddenly recalled a dream that he was in wartime Yugoslavia with his Betar friends, surrounded by German soldiers with guns threatening to kill them. "The same story now happened, but . . . not German soldiers around us but Jewish brothers, from the same blood. . . ."

"Palestine's roads," wrote journalist Arthur Koestler, who had arrived in Israel three weeks earlier, were "bristling with armed patrols." The *Palestine Post* reported "sten-gun patrols at every corner." Yigael Yadin, who described the Irgun men on board the *Altalena* as "enemies," commanded "Operation Purification" to cleanse the nation of Irgun contamination. Under wartime emergency regulations authorizing extralegal action, he ordered raids on Irgun bases and the homes of its activists. IDF assault units attacked Irgun headquarters in Tel Aviv, where two hundred commanders and soldiers were arrested and their weapons confiscated. Once again, as on the beaches of Kfar Vitkin and Tel Aviv, there was no resistance. Five senior Irgun commanders — Lankin, Meridor, Hillel Kook, Moshe Hason and Bezalel Amitzur — were held in detention for two months.

BROTHERS AT WAR

At a Cabinet meeting, Ben-Gurion encountered sharp criticism of government decisions. To the four religious Zionist ministers, the sinking of the ship was both undemocratic and illegal. Rabbi Fishman-Maimon and Moshe Shapira from the Mizrahi party demanded the immediate release of Irgun prisoners. Interior Minister Gruenbaum proposed a judicial inquiry accompanied by the establishment of a committee to determine how best to maintain law and order, preserve the unity of the Israel Defense Forces, and accelerate the pardoning of prisoners "to avoid civil war." Once his proposal was accepted, Ministers Fishman-Maimon and Shapira resigned, while Gruenbaum and Peretz Bernstein remained to challenge Ben-Gurion's actions.

Following the impassioned Cabinet discussion about the *Altalena*, ministers considered "whether Jerusalem was part of the State of Israel." Linkage between the *Altalena* and Jerusalem was hardly coincidental. If Jerusalem indeed lay outside the boundaries of the nascent Jewish state, as the UN had proposed, then Irgun fighters there were not covered by Ben-Gurion's insistence upon dismantling its separate fighting force. So, at least, Begin had believed their agreement stipulated. But Jerusalem, Ben-Gurion asserted, remained "under the authority of the government" — "though not, I regret to say, the Old City."

In reality, however, its authority was extremely tenuous. Cut off from the government and general staff in Tel Aviv, Jerusalem had not been visited by a government official in five weeks. As Yitzhak Ben-Zvi (who would become Israel's second president) described the dire situation, Jerusalem faced not only constant enemy attack but "economic collapse." Hunger and looting were widespread, and despairing Jewish residents were fleeing to safety outside the city. Rabbi Berlin was convinced that "we cannot control Jerusalem."

Zerah Warhaftig, one of the signers of the Proclamation of Independence, reported: "We felt that we had been forgotten." Another minister cited "a spirit of defeatism among the poor Jews of Jerusalem." But Ben-Gurion affirmed that Jerusalem "was under the jurisdiction of the Jewish Government to the same extent as Tel

Aviv." The next day, clearly chastened by what he had heard, he "went up to Jerusalem." It was too late. The ancient Old City had been irretrievably lost and, with the attack on the *Altalena*, the Irgun had no weapons with which to continue the fight.

At a meeting of the Provisional State Council, with all thirty-seven members present, Ben-Gurion summarized the "rebellion." He praised Commander Even for acting "with a maximum of efficiency and a minimum of bloodshed." The terms of surrender accepted by the Irgun at Kfar Vitkin had required the cessation of all "hostile acts" and surrender of all weapons and military equipment. "This appeared to be the end of the Etzel revolt," Ben-Gurion had concluded. But the *Altalena* had "slipped away."

Arriving in Tel Aviv, "it refused to comply with our orders to leave the city and turn over its cargo of weapons to the authorities. The Government had previously decided that if this was not done, force would be used against the vessel, and so it was." Describing the episode as "an armed uprising" fed by "the chicanery of the dissidents," Ben-Gurion warned: "The arrogant action of armed gangs inside the country gravely endangers our ability to defend our future and the future of the entire Jewish people." The army and the nation, he insisted, must "uproot this evil."

When debate began, the nagging internal divisions within the Zionist movement — between left and right, religious and secular — erupted vehemently. Foreign Minister Shertok asked sharply: "Why did Etzel refuse to turn over the ship and its weapons to the Government? Was there any justification for its refusal?" He concluded bluntly: "Anarchy will not be permitted in this country." Rabbi Berlin (Mizrahi) conceded that once a rebellion occurred the government had both the right and duty to suppress it "with all the power at its disposal." But "the killing of Jews by other Jews" was deeply unsettling. For this Ben-Gurion was to blame: he had acted "solely on his own initiative" and "his actions were excessive."

On the Zionist left, Zvi Luria (Mapam) vigorously condemned the Irgun: "Who ambushed and murdered people? Why were the weapons not turned over immediately?" He commended the government for its "firm stand" against "an organization which has challenged the very sovereignty of the State of Israel and the authority of the Israel Defense Forces." A colleague added: "Today we have a State which enjoys complete sovereignty; there can be no compromise on this point. There cannot be several armies in one country." By a vote of 24-4, the Council adopted a resolution expressing "its support of the actions of the Government aimed at preventing Etzel from bringing in weapons without Government permission."

At a press conference, Galili (according to the newspaper *Davar*) expressed the government's "surprise" at the imminent arrival of the *Altalena*. He blamed the crisis on "the grave fact of a boat's arriving on the shores of the country during the truce without our prior knowledge, without our being asked, without our agreeing." But the arrival of the *Altalena* hardly was a surprise to Galili (or Ben-Gurion). One week earlier, in his briefing to the military command before the *Altalena* reached shore, Galili had acknowledged: "We knew the arms were due to arrive. . . ." (His contradictory statements to the military and to journalists surfaced only years later, in Dan Even's Foreword to a history of the Alexandroni Brigade.) Galili would subsequently assert (in an article in *Ma'ariv*) that he had "reported fully" to Ben-Gurion and Defense Minister Eshkol, "at each stage, both by word of mouth, and in writing, about the meetings with Irgun leaders."

With the Irgun command still in shock over the attack and its losses, Lehi leader Israel Eldad visited Begin in his fortified Tel Aviv headquarters. Begin's voice, he recalled, sounded "broken." Eldad insisted that no allegiance was owed "to this kind of 'government.'" He suggested that the Irgun and Lehi relocate to Jerusalem and continue the struggle for a "free Judea" there. Begin was too emotionally depleted even to respond.

Two days later, senior military officers took an oath of allegiance to the State of Israel. At the conclusion of the ceremony, Ben-Gurion declared: "The Oath that you have just taken links you with the Hebrew commanders from the days of Joshua, the fighting

CIVIL WAR?

and liberating Judges, the Kings of Israel and Judea, Nehemia, the Maccabees, the heroes of the war against the Romans in the days of the Second Temple. . . ." Jewish national independence had finally been restored. But only weeks after its creation, the groundless hatred between Jews that had undermined Jewish sovereignty in the 1st century hovered menacingly over the State of Israel.

In mid-September, Lehi fighters assassinated Count Folke Bernadotte, the United Nations Security Council mediator for the Middle East, in Jerusalem. His proposal for an eviscerated Jewish state had included an Arab-Jewish union with Arab sovereignty over Jerusalem, Israeli surrender of the vast Negev desert, and unlimited Jewish immigration for two years to be controlled thereafter by its dominant Arab partner. Once again, as he had done after Lehi agents assassinated Lord Moyne, Ben-Gurion turned his fury on the Irgun, giving it twenty-four hours to relinquish all weapons and dissolve itself "unconditionally." If it did not, he warned, the army would act "with all the means at its disposal."

Begin accepted the ultimatum; on September 20 the Irgun ceased to exist as a separate military organization. Within months, it would transform itself into the Herut (Freedom) party, choosing to pursue its political objectives through the electoral process. Begin, Lankin, Kook, Merlin and Eri Jabotinsky were among the fourteen Herut members elected to the first Knesset in January 1949.

Not long after the *Altalena* battle 21-year-old Rafael Khirs, from a Zionist Orthodox family in Transylvania (whose closest relatives had perished in the Holocaust), expressed his anguish and rage:

> We embarked on our voyage
>
> To suffer and fight for you.
>
> We brought you revolutionary courage
>
> And an arms-ship to liberate you.
>
> For years in Europe
>
> We toiled without pause
>
> To bring you Altalena

BROTHERS AT WAR

> The fruit of our labors.
>
> And how you received us!
>
> God
>
> We'll never forget!
>
> Of brothers-in-arms we dreamt
>
> But encountered the cannon blast.
>
> And although they sank Altalena
>
> Raise your head high soldiers.
>
> To the whole of Eretz Yisrael
>
> We remain forever loyal.

Less than four months later, Khirs (along with sixteen other *Altalena* fighters) proved his loyalty when he was killed in battle defending the State of Israel.

For several weeks, young boys swam out to the *Altalena* to gather rifles whose barrels had been twisted by the explosions and fire. Uri Dan, one of them, still recalled fifty-five years later "how my heart broke when I saw the burning ship." The war between brothers was over. But sorrowful memories and acrimonious allegations from the *Altalena* tragedy would continue to surface long after those two terrible days in June 1948.

Photographs

1. David Ben-Gurion reading the Proclamation of Independence, May 14, 1948. Photo by Kluger Zoltan. Reprinted with permission of the National Photo Collection, State of Israel.

2. On board the *Altalena*. Photograph by David Taggar.

3. Monroe Fein, Captain of the *Altalena*. Courtesy of the Jabotinsky Institute in Israel.

4. Eliahu Lankin, Irgun Commander on the *Altalena*. Courtesy of the Jabotinsky Institute in Israel.

5. On board the *Altalena*. Reprinted with permission of U.S. Holocaust Memorial Museum.

6. Menachem Begin reviewing Irgun fighters. Photo by David Csasznik.

7. *Altalena* Burning. Photograph by Hans Pinn. Reprinted with permission of the National Photo Collection, State of Israel.

8. *Altalena* burning and rescue attempts. Photograph by Robert Capa. Copyright © Magnum Photos, New York. Reproduced under license with Magnum Photos.

Chapter 4
Competing Truths

Arab nations were unrelenting in their refusal to permit a Jewish state to exist in their midst. The fighting that accompanied their consuming determination to obliterate Israel would claim more than six thousand Israeli lives — one per cent of its population — and drive hundreds of thousands of Palestinian Arabs from their homes. But during the ceasefire that began on June 11th the Arab threat was momentarily overshadowed by the violent confrontation over the *Altalena*. With sixteen Irgun fighters and three Israeli soldiers killed and dozens wounded during twenty-four hours of fierce fighting on two beaches, it was an Israeli tragedy. No sooner had Jewish national sovereignty been restored than the unity needed to sustain it unraveled. Why?

The battles at Kfar Vitkin and Tel Aviv climaxed the persistent struggle within Zionism over political legitimacy. They raised fundamental issues of governance: When does the exercise of power become arbitrary and unjust? Is there a higher law than the law of the state? Who decides when to obey — or disobey? Does the end justify the means? The *Altalena* episode provokes more specific questions: Was there "a mutiny on the right," in "open defiance of the laws of the land" (as Ben-Gurion biographer Michael Bar-Zohar asserted)? Was the use of force to suppress it justified, or excessive? Did Ben-Gurion so misjudge, mistrust, or distort the intentions of his despised political opponent Menachem Begin as to leave no alternative to needless and excessive violence?

Whose decisions were praiseworthy, politically and morally: the Haganah and Palmach soldiers who fired on other Jews, or those who refused to shoot? As their testimony vividly and painfully revealed, some soldiers were deeply torn — then and long afterward — between their obligation to obey orders and their excruciating pangs of conscience because the designated targets were their Jewish "brothers." For some, nothing worse could be imagined than *milchemet achim*, a "war of brothers."

Others experienced a wrenching stab of memory from Jewish antiquity. Confronting the horrific reality of Jews fighting (and killing) other Jews, anguished participants (and stunned witnesses) identified the conflict between the government and Irgun with the 1st century Jewish civil war so vividly described by Josephus. References to brotherly betrayal by Cain revealed how deeply and painfully the *Altalena* confrontation pierced Israeli memory.

By 1948 David Ben-Gurion and Menachem Begin had developed deep reciprocal mistrust, if not mutual loathing, from their years of struggle for a Jewish state. They personified the fierce, persistent conflict over Zionist ideological supremacy and political strategy. Irreconcilable differences over the Arlosoroff assassination, the transfer agreement, and responses to British policy in Palestine, with lingering memories from the Season, had nurtured animosity that burst forth with the arrival of the *Altalena*.

Begin's unrelenting determination to confront the British, with violent force if necessary, had not been popular in the weak and dependent Yishuv, especially among leaders on the political left. But to advance the cause of Jewish statehood, he knew, required driving the British from Palestine. The Irgun had occasionally chosen brutal methods: conspicuous among them, bombing the King David hotel and hanging the British sergeants. Yet nothing did more to undermine British rule and provoke its government to finally relinquish Mandatory authority than the high cost exacted by the Irgun for the continuing British presence in Palestine.

With independence, Begin believed that the arrival of desperately needed weapons and munitions would be recognized as an exemplary demonstration of patriotism. Here, after all, was a significant Irgun military contribution to the struggle for statehood — anything but an attempt to overthrow the government. Perhaps (as Eliahu Lankin eventually conceded) this was "naïve." Given Ben-Gurion's intolerance for dissent, the Irgun leader surely had reason to know better. But Begin yearned for the honor and respect that for so long had been denied to him and to his Irgun fighters. He badly misjudged Ben-Gurion's willingness to use force to have his way — not against the British but against his Zionist enemies.

By now Ben-Gurion and Begin, along with many *Altalena* passengers and crewmembers, Irgun fighters, and IDF soldiers have had their say — or chosen to remain silent. Journalists, biographers, and scholars have written about this most divisive and violent episode of internal conflict in Israeli history. Only the assassination in 1995 of Prime Minister Yitzhak Rabin — Palmach commander on the Tel Aviv beach that June day in 1948 — has cast as dark a shadow over the political culture of the Jewish state. But the battle did not end on the Tel Aviv beach. It remains a contested memory to this day. More than sixty years later, the *Altalena* continues to surface in Israeli consciousness — as a reminder, a lesson, a warning, or even — for some — an inspirational model.

An anguished Begin was the first to speak after the devastating attack. Born in 1913 in Brest-Litovsk, then under Russian rule, he had been educated in a religious Zionist school. Joining *Hashomer Hatzair*, the Socialist Zionist youth movement, he soon left it for Betar, its Revisionist counterpart. By his mid-twenties, after becoming a devoted disciple of Ze'ev Jabotinsky, he was chosen as the Betar leader for Poland and Czechoslovakia. After the Nazi invasion of Poland Begin fled to Lithuania where, following the Soviet invasion a year later, he was imprisoned for his Betar activities. Released from a labor camp he joined the Polish army, which dispatched his unit to Palestine. With the Irgun still in disarray after Jabotinsky's death in 1940, Begin became its commander.

Fiercely ideological, Begin was adored by his right-wing followers and loathed by his opponents on the left. He never lost his dream of a Jewish homeland in the entirety of Mandatory Palestine west of the Jordan River, if not also on the east bank, originally included within Palestine by the League of Nations. The perennial political outsider, Begin had survived the Season by hiding in disguise in his secret house on Habashan Street in Tel Aviv. Labeled by one of his biographers as "a courtly rabble-rouser," he could be unfailingly polite or scathing — at times verbose and emotional — but to his loyal followers, always inspirational. These attributes were vividly on display the evening after he was rowed ashore from the blazing *Altalena*, when he delivered an impassioned — critics said hysterical — radio address to the nation from Irgun headquarters.

The arrival of the *Altalena*, Begin insisted, was not "an act of provocation." Representatives of the Provisional Government had known about it for "at least four days" before the ship reached Kfar Vitkin. "To our great joy official and precise consent" had been granted; "the entire discussion was only concerning the allocation of the arms." Begin asked: "For years [the Irgun] had dreamed of these arms. . . . How could we not give [them] to our fighters in the army?" To be sure, there was "bitterness . . . deep within us" from the "dark and bitter days and nights when our men were tortured, beaten and given up to the British intelligence." But Irgun fighters had nonetheless joined the Israel Defense Forces with the assurance that they would be "under your command and fight the common foe at your command."

When his men came under fire at Kfar Vitkin, Begin explained, he had decided to sail to Tel Aviv to resolve the "snag in relations." But there, too, "fire was directed against Jews and they kept firing." Even the Arab Legion in the Old City of Jerusalem, he recounted scathingly, had respected a truce to remove wounded Jews. "Hebrew fighters killed," he lamented, "to make the man [Ben-Gurion] who has ever surrendered to the foreigner appear firm towards Jews." Although the government of Israel had honored truces demanded by the British, "here it was different. Here their force was directed against Jews and they kept firing without stop." Even with the *Altalena* ablaze, "they were firing at wounded men in the water . . . at the command of the head of your government."

With rising emotion that climaxed in choking rage and weeping, Begin asked: "What did the government hope to achieve by shelling the ship? Why was the cease-fire broken? Are not these arms needed by us all? Why did they not come to negotiate with us? They, who at the slightest beck and call run to negotiate with

COMPETING TRUTHS

[British Foreign Minister] Bevin? . . . Why did they behave in such a barbaric manner?" By sinking the *Altalena*, he claimed, the government had "lost its legitimacy." Accusing Ben-Gurion of a "crime," Begin nonetheless implored his loyal Irgun followers: "Raise not your hand against your brother. Not even today. . . . Simple Jews who give their all for their nation, we shall continue to love Israel and fight for it."

Perhaps Begin had clung too long to the naïve faith that fifteen years of conflict, and the deep chasm of suspicion that had opened between the government and the Irgun, could have been bridged if only he was given the opportunity to leave the ship in Tel Aviv to resolve the "snag in relations." His craving for legitimacy for the Irgun, and for government recognition of its contributions to the struggle for independence, may have blinded him to Ben-Gurion's relentless determination to resist any challenge, real or imagined, to his own authority.

But it was not merely a "snag." It was the final spasm of a rupture that already was far too severe to be so easily mended. Begin may have craved honor and respect, but Ben-Gurion demanded authority and power — and he was relentless in their pursuit. Begin failed to anticipate how Ben-Gurion would perceive and respond to a shipload of arms and munitions from his despised political enemy. Had Ben-Gurion "not been as suspicious as he was of the Irgun's subversive intentions," Begin wrote, "the lives of innocent Jews might have . . . been spared."

Begin's critics lacerated him for the anguished and tearful conclusion to his radio address. Such "soft emotionalism" seemed inappropriate, even unmanly, for a national leader. To an overwrought Haganah correspondent, Begin's radio speech was a reminder of "Hitler's harangues." Had Irgun men aboard the *Altalena* been allowed to land, they "would have constituted a graver threat to the continued existence of the Jewish State than all the armies of the Arab League combined."

In *The Revolt*, Begin responded to his critics: "There are tears of which no man need be ashamed. . . . As our revolt against the

[British] oppressor taught us, it is essential that blood should take the place of tears. And sometimes, as the *Altalena* taught us, it is essential that tears should take the place of blood." Once again, as he had during the Season, Begin demanded of his followers, even as they came under attack: no civil war. To the Irgun leader, the *Altalena* tragedy would remain "an extreme example of Ben-Gurion's arbitrariness and authoritarian tendencies." It would take two decades of wandering in the political wilderness, isolated and marginalized, before Begin's exile finally ended.

In his speech to the Provisional Council the next day, David Ben-Gurion strongly asserted his own version of what had happened, and why. Born in Poland in 1886, he immigrated to Palestine twenty years later. Expelled by Ottoman authorities in 1915 for his Zionist political activities, he lived in New York before joining the Jewish Legion of the British army during World War I. Returning to Palestine after the war, and with it the collapse of the Ottoman empire, Ben-Gurion launched his political career as a founder and then general secretary of the Zionist Labor Federation (*Histadrut*). From this position, his first base of political power, he asserted authority over Jewish workers in Palestine. By 1935, when he became chairman of the executive committee of the Jewish Agency, the governing body of the Yishuv, he was determined to expand and consolidate his own power until his consuming goal, Jewish statehood, was achieved.

Two weeks after the assassination of Lord Moyne in November 1944, Ben-Gurion addressed a *Histadrut* conference where he tarred the entire political right with the brush of terrorism. Although his primary target was Lehi, which bore sole responsibility for Moyne's murder, the only group he specifically named in his scathing condemnation was the Irgun, which posed the more menacing political challenge. Ben-Gurion's speech offered a concise preview of the explanation and self-justification that he would repeat to the Provisional Council nearly four years later, after the *Altalena* confrontation.

COMPETING TRUTHS

For Ben-Gurion in 1944, the alternatives were unmistakably clear: "political, Zionist, resistance" or "terrorism." He railed against "murder and robbery, blackmail and theft," claiming that unjustified crimes were being "committed in the name of Zionism." Unidentified people, he warned, "wrap their wrongdoing in a cloak of nationalism," posing the stark choice between "violence and repression, or constitutional liberties." Gangs of "maniacs," he declared furiously, "murder Englishmen and Jews with the same fanatic zeal."

Perceiving "a state of war" among citizens of the Yishuv, Ben-Gurion had demanded "a purge of terrorists from our ranks." He advised landlords to evict "contaminated tenants." Even young students who distributed or posted the handbills of his political enemies, Ben-Gurion declared, were guilty of a "traitorous felony" warranting expulsion from school. (In May 1947 just such a student, 16-year-old Alexander Rubowitz, was seized by a British police officer while posting Lehi notices in Jerusalem and murdered in the Judean hills.) Ben-Gurion pledged Zionist cooperation with British authorities to "uproot terrorism."

In his lengthy and impassioned speech to the Provisional Council after the *Altalena* battle, Ben-Gurion reiterated the dangers of internal discord and justified the necessity of military force. If Begin, in his radio address, had condemned the government for declaring war on the Irgun, Ben-Gurion indicted the Irgun for provoking civil war. Vigorously defending his own actions, his opening sentence referred to "an attempt, pregnant with calamity, by the Irgun Zvai Leumi to wound the unity and sovereignty of the State, its military power and its international status." The establishment of the Israel Defense Forces (at a time when the Haganah, Palmach, Irgun, and Lehi still retained their separate identities as fighting units) had explicitly forbidden "the formation or maintenance of any armed forces" other than by the new army. Ben-Gurion emphasized the necessity of "a united army, loyal to one Government" for resistance against the foreign enemies that Israel confronted.

BROTHERS AT WAR

The government, he asserted, had made "concessions" to the Irgun by permitting its fighters to join the IDF in separate units that would enable them to preserve their distinctive identity. In return, however, the Irgun was required to "cease to exist as a military unit," surrender its weapons, and terminate its independent efforts to procure military supplies. But "the Irgun and its Command continued to operate; arms and equipment were still obtained independently, and the sources therof denied to the Army." That, Ben-Gurion claimed, was "the dark background . . . of the grievous doings" at Kfar Vitkin and Tel Aviv.

The Prime Minister vigorously defended his decision "to break the dissident organization" with military force. By bringing the *Altalena*, a "mutinous craft," to Israel the Irgun had disregarded its own commitments and defied the "statutes" of the nation. "No State can countenance private citizens or organizations thus importing . . . even the tiniest armory, much less the wholesale consignment of rifles and machine-guns that the Irgun tried to land this time." Such "indiscipline and faithlessness," Ben-Gurion asserted, "is a frightful threat to the State and might set the fuse for a disastrous civil war." Once the Irgun refused to yield control of the ship to the government, "my duty was clear. The safety of the State must be preserved, the law carried out — and I knew that only by force could it be done."

"Was it not enough to undergo the murderous ordeal of Arab hatred," Ben-Gurion asked, "that this bitter aftertaste of blood should be proffered us by fellow-Jews?" With Israel confronting a fight for survival, he warned, "armed revolt . . . spells ruin of the Yishuv's strength to defend itself and its future." The existence of "rebel gangs" could not be tolerated. Had the weapons on board the *Altalena* "fallen into the hands of terrorists, . . . they might have wrecked the State and the freedom of its Yishuv." An "armed minority" had usurped the monopoly of the state on the exercise of force; its continued existence assured further bloodshed. "More than once has the Irgun spilled Jewish blood, and the blood of others; these things must not happen again."

COMPETING TRUTHS

The Irgun, Ben-Gurion asserted, "brought catastrophe about," while "the Government, at whatever cost, brought about deliverance." He had demanded of the Irgun only that it surrender its arms and military equipment, with its members reporting for military service like anyone else. There would be "no special agreements, simply enforcement of the law made by the State for every citizen without discrimination." Ben-Gurion conceded: "It is tragic that we should have to use force against fellow-Jews. But it is a far greater tragedy that they should have forced us to, that they should have broken their promises and belied their declarations."

Had the Irgun retained the weapons that were on board the *Altalena*, Ben-Gurion warned, it could have persisted in "domestic terrorism, attacking and even killing, as they killed before. . . ." In language echoing his 1944 speech, he insisted that the state would not tolerate a "gang of terrorists," functioning as "a private army with private arms." Given the evident dangers — "a truce infringed, our sovereignty risked" — he insisted that "to burn this ship was the most loyal service we could render the Yishuv." In his concluding peroration, long remembered, he exulted: "Blessed be the cannon that sunk that ship. [It] is worthy of being mounted in the new Temple when it is built." It became known, almost immediately, as "*ha-totach ha-kadosh*" ("the holy cannon").

Triumphantly asserting state power — and, implicitly, his own — Ben-Gurion not only challenged the actions of his political opponents but their legitimacy. The Irgun, which he labeled "detesting," was an untrustworthy and defiant "gang of terrorists." It had "usurped" power that belonged to the state and, by extension, to Ben-Gurion as its leader. It had been prepared to plunge the new nation into a civil war while incurring the wrath of external authorities (once the British, now the United Nations) to advance its own partisan interests. He warned against a society "in which there is no single authority, no single arsenal, no single discipline." The State had been "forced" to attack in self-preservation. "It was better that the ship was burned."

BROTHERS AT WAR

Yet there were conspicuous contradictions and omissions — indeed, mistruths — in Ben-Gurion's fiery self-justification. He wrote in his unpublished diaries that Begin's "tragic and despicable, but failed attempt at a *putsch*" constituted an attack on Israeli democracy. But his insistence upon Begin's intention to overthrow the government, reiterated by his loyal followers, was unsupported by even a shred of evidence, then or since. Ben-Gurion also claimed that he had learned about the *Altalena* only two days before its arrival at Kfar Vitkin. If true, this meant that his own negotiators, especially Yisrael Galili, had not kept him informed about what they had learned as early as their meeting with Begin on May 15th, and again in mid-June. Galili subsequently rejected this allegation.

Ben-Gurion himself had authorized — indeed, commanded — the landing at Kfar Vitkin. The government had knowingly approved the arrival of weapons and munitions, in contravention of the UN ceasefire. His denial of any agreement to permit 20 per cent of the arms to be funneled to Irgun fighters in Jerusalem ignored the June 3rd understanding reached by Begin and Galili in the presence of IDF commander Yigael Yadin. "One thing I must deny," Ben-Gurion strongly asserted in his most egregious misstatement, was that "shots were fired at those who abandoned ship after it caught fire and swam ashore." But even Palmach soldiers (including Yitzhak Rabin), to say nothing of observers and journalists on the scene, witnessed and explicitly stated otherwise. Photographic evidence, showing bullet splashes in the water, contradicted Ben-Gurion's claim.

Ben-Gurion's guiding political philosophy, "statism," required a strong central government with power firmly consolidated in his hands. He would control all the competing Zionist factions, marginalize their disparate ideologies and, above all, eradicate their military forces. Serving simultaneously as Prime Minister and Defense Minister, Ben-Gurion had little, if any, tolerance for political opposition. Only months after the *Altalena* crisis, apprehensive that the far left Mapam party might seize power with the help of the Palmach, he forced the elite military unit to relinquish its separate identity and merge into the IDF. His peremptory order prompted some of the most experienced Palmach officers to leave the military and return to their kibbutzim.

"Among us," Ben-Gurion told his own Mapai Central Committee a year later, "the disputes are not like those of more-or-less normal people, but like those of zealots." He was widely praised (then and since) for imposing state authority on those who dared to challenge it. "He thereby secured Israel's lasting democracy," historian Anita Shapira has written. But the question remains: was Ben-Gurion himself to be counted among the "zealots" whom he so furiously despised, denounced — and attacked?

His Interior Minister, Yitzhak Gruenbaum, had tried in vain to find a compromise that would avoid bloodshed. Only two weeks earlier, in a meeting of the government commission established to analyze the conduct of the war, he had delineated Ben-Gurion's unyielding obstinacy: "He crushes all obstacles and all opposition. . . . He cannot bear other opinions that conflict with his own." Gruenbaum had urged "some mechanism . . . which will constrain those defects, deficiencies and dangers presented by him." It was a prescient warning, but when his authority was challenged — as the *Altalena* episode demonstrated — Ben-Gurion could not be constrained.

Israeli journalist Shabtai Teveth, author of a massive biography of Ben-Gurion during the pre-state years, has cited "the establishment of authority" as his "great life work." Unrelenting in his determination to restore the national sovereignty that the Jewish people had lacked in exile for nearly two thousand years, Ben-Gurion often displayed what even his stanch admirer Teveth identified as "imperviousness to anyone who stood in his way." A man of "impulsive outbursts and . . . daring leaps," biographer Bar-Zohar concedes that he was, by nature, "authoritarian." Left-wing Israeli historian Tom Segev has concluded: Ben-Gurion's "giant shadow possessed certain quasi-totalitarian characteristics." They never were more tragically on display than during the *Altalena* crisis.

BROTHERS AT WAR

It is revealing that once Ben-Gurion addressed the Provisional Council on June 23rd, virtually no other voices from within the government or military were heard in public — not then and only rarely thereafter. His intolerance of dissent hardly was a secret; his underlings either bowed to his will or departed. Labor party ministers, leaders and military officers maintained public silence, burying any disagreements to close ranks behind their leader. Others quietly exited. After a dispute with Ben-Gurion, Yigael Yadin, who commanded the Israel Defense Forces during the Independence War, soon turned to archeology. He remained silent about the *Altalena*. In *The Making of Israel's Army* (1970), Yigal Allon omitted any mention of the Tel Aviv battle that he had commanded or the cannon whose firing he had ordered.

It took a surprising twist of historical irony, twenty-nine years (almost to the day) after the *Altalena* battle, for Yitzhak Rabin to speak in public about the *Altalena*. When Menachem Begin succeeded him as prime minister in 1977, Rabin wrote in his memoir, "I found myself awash in memories." He remained "reconciled to Ben-Gurion's decision to maintain law and order in the state that has just been born, and to prevent a breach in the civil and military authority of the state." But he acknowledged "the residue of hatred of the people of the Palmach and the Haganah" toward Begin and the Irgun.

Perhaps, Rabin conceded, Begin "never intended more than to provision the fighters with additional weapons and ammunition. But while the events were unfolding, I was convinced that the IZL's intentions were far-reaching — to seize control of Israel by force." In his interview for Ilana Tzur's film "Altalena," one year before his assassination nearly twenty years later, Rabin still recalled "a feeling of a military *putsch*."

In sharp contrast to the silence, or long-delayed justification, from Ben-Gurion's loyalists, the flood of Irgun responses, both immediately and subsequently, reflected its entirely different organizational structure — and the deeply felt need of its leaders to defend their decisions and actions. Unlike the Mapai-ruled government,

COMPETING TRUTHS

with power concentrated in Ben-Gurion's hands, Irgun leadership, geographically divided between Palestine and Paris, was diffused — and occasionally contentious. Coordination was problematic, as the *Altalena*'s departure from Port-du-Bouc and Begin's inability to communicate with Fein and Lankin, had demonstrated. On board the ship, commander Lankin was in charge; indeed, he overrode Begin's explicit instructions to delay arrival and made the crucial decision to continue the journey. The diffusion — and occasional confusion — of Irgun leadership, if nothing else, made a planned *putsch* impossible, if not inconceivable.

The shock of the government's violent response to the arrival of the *Altalena* and the loss of sixteen of its fighting men produced an outpouring of grief and rage that, for some, would never recede. From the day the ship was attacked, Irgun loyalists furiously challenged Ben-Gurion's decision, explanation and justification. An official Irgun statement, issued immediately afterward, condemned "the barbaric behaviour of the lunatic 'dictator.'" Ben-Gurion, it charged, had "established a regime of tyranny." In language laced with rage — mixing memories of the Season with Holocaust metaphors — the statement blamed "a government of criminal oppressors, who, if they continue to reign, will do so with the help of concentration camps, torture cells and hangings." With unrestrained fury, it revoked an order to Irgun soldiers to enlist in, and swear allegiance to, the Israel Defense Forces.

Shmuel Katz, a member of the Irgun High Command who did not arrive in Israel until the day after the battle, condemned a "plot" by the government "that only narrowly failed in its Fascistic objectives of political murder and personal assassination." Irgun loyalists in England excoriated Ben-Gurion for his "Gestapo methods." The American branch of Brit Trumpeldor, founded by Jabotinsky to memorialize the Zionist martyr of the 1920s, castigated Ben-Gurion's "storm troopers" and "Jewish Quislings."

Lehi leader Israel Eldad angrily dismissed the claim that the *Altalena* was "a rebel ship being used for a *putsch*." He insisted that those who propagated such a "libel" were "weaned on the same dark blood as the forgers of the earlier Arlosoroff libel." The attack on the ship expressed nothing more than Ben-Gurion's "desire to eliminate . . . a competitor for power" and preserve "the existing regime." But government legitimacy, Eldad insisted, is undermined once it "refuses to stop before the border called: 'Shedding brothers' blood.'" In the end, he believed that Ben-Gurion's command to attack was "an old score being settled" with the pre-state underground movements. Eldad bitterly recalled "the faces of Palmach men and women who danced and sang in the cars returning from the slaughter, as they drove down Ben Yehuda and Allenby Streets in Tel Aviv. . . . I heard with my own ears Jewish girls laughing over the blood."

Several days after the battle an Irgun radio broadcast lamented that its fighters had been killed "in order to make the man who has ever surrendered to the foreigner appear firm toward Jews." Its allegations included the claim, based on "a top secret intelligence report of absolute reliability," that the government had initiated the *Altalena* confrontation to conceal secret negotiations with King Abdullah of Jordan. If successful, they would have required far-reaching land concessions from Israel, if not its virtual abdication of statehood within the Arab-Jewish federation favored by the king.

Tempers also flared in the United States. Louis Bromfield, chairman of the American League for a Free Palestine, accused Ben-Gurion and his "henchmen" of seeking "to liquidate and physically annihilate" the Irgun. But *Hashomer Hatzair,* the Zionist youth movement, circulated an open letter thanking Ben-Gurion for destroying "the ship loaded with arms for an Irgun coup d'état." Support for Begin, it warned, assured "support for gangsterism well-schooled in the tenets of the Nazi primer." *Time* magazine berated Begin, his "bullyboys," and "terrorists" for provoking "a short, sharp civil war of Jew against Jew." Influential American Jews worked discreetly behind the scenes to marginalize the Irgun. Henry Morgenthau, Jr., formerly President Roosevelt's Secretary of the Treasury and a post-war fund-raiser for Jewish refugee causes, tried to discourage financial support for the Irgun, whose actions harmed

Israel's "prestige" — and might, therefore, jeopardize the security of American Jews.

At the United Nations, the Arab High Committee for Palestine submitted a statement asserting that "the spectacular beach battle" in Israel was nothing more than "a mock fight intended to camouflage the arrival of arms on board the *Altalena* in violation of the ceasefire." The Haganah and Irgun, it claimed, had "staged" the conflict "in order to throw dust in the eyes of the Security Council and world public opinion." In his response Israeli representative Aubrey Eban claimed that his new and precarious nation had displayed its ability to assert "internal authority and its respect for international obligation, even in the cruelest and most poignant of circumstances." A report from the United Nations Mediator noted with satisfaction that the Israeli Government had taken "strong police action" against the Irgun.

Irgun loyalists were not alone in berating Ben-Gurion for his decision to use military force. Three days later Arthur Koestler, in Tel Aviv as a reporter, filed his own account with the *Manchester Guardian*. A resident of Palestine and follower of Jabotinsky during the 1920s, he subsequently became a disillusioned Communist who wrote the stunning *Darkness at Noon* to expose the horrors of totalitarianism. Koestler returned to Palestine in 1944. He met secretly with Begin, then hiding from the British (and the Haganah), but his efforts failed to persuade the Irgun leader to moderate his militancy.

Koestler was not convinced by the government's protestations of surprise over the arrival of the *Altalena*. Its preparations for sailing, he wrote, had been "an open secret in Tel Aviv for the last four weeks." The government "seemed more concerned with settling old accounts than with national unity." Foreign Minister Shertok's insistence that it had responded appropriately to Irgun defiance did not persuade Koestler, who described the bloody confrontation as the "welcome pretext for the liquidation of an unruly opposition group." The aftermath of the attack on the *Altalena*, with its "savage street and beach fighting," reminded him ("ominously") of Barcelona in 1937 during the Spanish Civil War. He asserted what Ben-Gurion, in his address to the Provisional Council, had denied: while the *Altalena* was ablaze, with its white surrender flag raised, IDF soldiers on the beach had continued to shoot at Irgun men who were desperately swimming ashore.

The government, Koestler claimed, was "obsessed with asserting its authority." Had it only "kept its head," the weapons aboard the *Altalena* would have been available once fighting resumed against Arab invaders. Instead, "like a young school teacher facing an unruly class," Ben-Gurion had reverted to "draconian measures." Yet to be elected by voters, the government "is displaying embryonic tendencies toward dictatorship." In an ensuing August meeting that Koestler recounted in his diary, Undersecretary of Defense Levi Eshkol reiterated "the necessity of asserting the authority of the state." He insisted: "Had we not done it this time, they would have brought more ships with more arms for themselves and finally there would have been a *putsch*."

Koestler's diary entries constituted a serious indictment of the Ben-Gurion government. Its "provocative ultimatum" (at Kfar Vitkin), combined with the revocation of previous assurances that a percentage of the arms on board the *Altalena* would go to Irgun fighters in Jerusalem, had "set a trap for Etzel." Koestler rejected Ben-Gurion's claim that he had been "forced" to use military power. Based on what he had witnessed in Tel Aviv, and his interview with Eshkol, Koestler concluded that the government had ordered the attack, even destroying desperately needed military supplies, because it "so badly wanted to avoid giving Begin the credit for bringing them."

Memoirs from Irgun leaders expanded the indictment. Five years after the confrontation Begin published *The Revolt*. Primarily the story of the prolonged Irgun struggle against British Mandatory rule in Palestine, it also included his account of the *Altalena* crisis. Despite "a sinister plot" by the government to destroy political opposition, the Irgun had remained steadfast in its determination "to avoid bloody civil war at all costs." As proof, Begin retraced his futile attempts to warn the *Altalena* not to land, followed by his prompt notification of its location and military cargo to Israeli security officers. The government's response, conveyed by Galili, had been to bring the ship to shore as quickly as possible. "Anxiety gave way to joy," Begin recalled. "The burden of responsibility had been taken off our shoulders." Government and Irgun representatives had "decided jointly" where the *Altalena* would land.

In the negotiations with government representatives Begin had been informed by Galili that the Department of Security had agreed to the Irgun proposal that twenty per cent of its military supplies would go to its fighting units in Jerusalem. Begin claimed that no agreement had been reached on the distribution of arms to Irgun soldiers elsewhere. Had the Irgun succeeded in unloading the ship, he claimed, "all of [the munitions] would have gone into the hands of the unified army. . . ." Begin insisted that the Irgun had not demanded weapons from the *Altalena* "'for ourselves,' as the inventors of the 'armed revolt' myth alleged." He berated the Ben-Gurion government for "fearful deeds" that demonstrated its "plan to rid itself of what it imagined was a serious political rivalry. It was more than sufficient to create a civil war." But the Irgun had pledged: "In no circumstances will we use arms against our fellow Jews." And it had honored that pledge.

Nearly twenty years later, in an article in *Ma'ariv*, Begin would claim that "a man high up in the State, one of the people closest to Ben-Gurion," had told him that the Prime Minister had been "deceived" about Irgun intentions. But Yisrael Galili, the prime suspect, rejected Begin's assertion. Interviewed by a journalist from *Yediot Aharonot*, Galili insisted: "There was no detail concerning the contacts with the IZL, at any level, which was not brought to the full and immediate knowledge of the Minister of Defense [Ben-Gurion]."

Even before Begin's memoir appeared, Eliahu Lankin had published *The Story of the Commander of the Altalena*, his own vivid account of the journey of the doomed ship. Lankin commanded operations on board from the moment it left Port-du-Bouc until it was evacuated under fire in Tel Aviv. (Subsequently elected to the first Knesset, he soon left politics to study and practice law. After Begin became prime minister in 1977, he appointed Lankin as Ambassador to South Africa.) Lankin's Epilogue to the English edition, published in 1992, presented his rebuttal to "the strident voice of government accusations against the Irgun," which the Israeli press had so faithfully reiterated. In what resembled a succinct legal brief, he sharply challenged government allegations against the Irgun: concealing information about the ship; violating the cease-fire and government agreements; "refusing to submit to the discipline of the State"; and "conspiring to overturn the government by force."

Lankin disputed Ben-Gurion's claim to the Provisional Council on June 23rd that he had only learned about the ship a few days before the *Altalena* reached Kfar Vitkin. To the contrary: the Irgun had disclosed its plans to government representatives as early as the May 15th meeting. Negotiations over the distribution of weapons had begun on June 15th, when Begin informed Galili and Eshkol that the *Altalena* had departed for Israel. The ceasefire notwithstanding, Arabs and Israelis alike were violating its terms. Indeed, on the very day the *Altalena* arrived at Kfar Vitkin, a Haganah ship (the *Inco*) unloaded a shipment of arms at Bat Yam. Government accusations against the Irgun, Lankin insisted, represented "a transparent double standard."

The government (in its statement of June 21st) had asserted that Irgun leaders, when "asked to submit to the discipline of the State," had refused to recognize its authority. Indeed, Begin had disobeyed the order of Commander Even to surrender weapons from the *Altalena* within ten minutes. But Begin, Lankin claimed, "did not regard this ultimatum seriously" and had sent Yaakov Meridor, his deputy, to discuss it with Even. The request for a meeting went unanswered. "At best," Lankin claimed, "the ultimatum was a misunderstanding; at worst, it was a provocation." It was Lankin's weakest point of rebuttal, perhaps reflecting his disbelief — or Begin's — that Ben-Gurion would actually wage war against fellow Jews.

COMPETING TRUTHS

"The accusation of a conspiracy to overthrow the Government of the State of Israel," Lankin vigorously asserted, was "the most vicious and the least credible of the claims" leveled against the Irgun. Despite Ben-Gurion's aggressive hostility during the Season, "the Irgun was always determined in its policies and actions to avoid fratricidal civil war." Although the Irgun and Begin were castigated, in 1948 and long afterward, for conspiring to overthrow the government, the notion of "a planned coup," Lankin wrote with evident anger, was an "outrageous accusation" that was "ridiculously incongruent with the facts."

The Irgun, Lankin asserted, had provided the government with advance information about the *Altalena*, its weapons inventory, and its date of departure from France. When the ship arrived, it had landed at "a location chosen by the Government." Its nine hundred fighters, "whose task supposedly was to take over the government by force, were unarmed." They made no attempt to distribute the weapons, packed in sealed crates, among themselves. Indeed, they were almost immediately transported from the ship to prepare for enlistment in the army. By the time the *Altalena* reached Tel Aviv, only "some tens of Irgun men" remained on board, while the beach was "held firmly" by the Palmach. "How much of a threat of 'overthrow by force,'" Lankin asked, could they have presented to the government?

Lankin remained convinced, more than forty years later, of "Ben-Gurion's determination to destroy the Irgun opposition as a significant element in the political life of the State." The *Altalena* confrontation, he asserted, was Ben-Gurion's "well-planned provocation." Simultaneously serving as Prime Minister and Defense Minister, he controlled "the Army, the press, and all other instruments of government." Determined "to retain the power in his hands [Ben-Gurion] took full political advantage of this psychological moment." In a crisis at a critical time, when the fate of Israel hung in the balance, "the nation did not dare not to believe him."

Yitzhaq Ben-Ami, one of the Bergson Boys, also published an account of the confrontation. Born in Palestine, as a young man and self-described "political neophyte" he had attended the trial of the accused murderers of Chaim Arlosoroff. Active in fund-raising organizations that subsidized immigration for Jewish refugees, Ben-Ami assumed diaspora leadership roles during the war years. Involved in planning for the *Altalena* expedition since early in 1947, he described the ship in his memoir as "our life-saving gift to our people. . . . But when we reached our brothers, they destroyed the gifts we brought them and tried to destroy us as well." He concluded sorrowfully: "The curse of '*Sinat Achim*' [brotherly hatred] has not been lifted from Israel. Once again, while the enemy was battering the walls, Jewish weapons were raised by brother against brother, to the everlasting shame of all of us."

The story of the *Altalena* has remained sharply contested ever since. Ben-Gurion and his political allies, Anita Shapira has written, "regarded its outcome as a miraculous deliverance for the Jewish state." His defenders invariably embraced the imperative of asserting national authority as the overriding justification for his actions. He was depicted as a bold commander who took the steps necessary to assure Israel's survival as an independent democratic state. Moving quickly past the misguided *Altalena* challenge, he confronted the urgent tasks of winning the war and building a nation.

To Begin's defenders and Irgun loyalists, however, Ben-Gurion had committed "a reprehensible abuse of state power": at best, it was "a tragic misunderstanding"; at worst, "a treacherous trap . . . to liquidate his IZL rivals once and for all." It exemplified his "arbitrariness and authoritarian tendencies"; rather than negotiate, or enlist mediators, he had chosen "to sanctify war." Future Defense Minister Moshe Arens, who left the United States in 1948 to join the Irgun, insisted that it was "a totally inexcusable partisan act to fire on a ship that brought guns and soldiers at the most critical time of the War of Independence."

The *Altalena* continued to punctuate Israeli politics, if only sporadically. Calls in the Knesset for a parliamentary committee of inquiry to reexamine the confrontation were rejected by the government. But Menachem Begin neither forgot nor forgave. Addressing

COMPETING TRUTHS

the Knesset in 1959, he referred to the government attack as a "desecration," asking: "Was there ever such an atrocity as this in Israel?" Not until 1965, on the eve of national elections, was there a perceptible softening of Ben-Gurion's fury toward Begin. The former prime minister publicly endorsed a commission of inquiry, conceding "Perhaps I was mistaken."

Historical memory is always reconstructed with scattered shards from the past, scrutinized and reinterpreted over time. The present is inevitably the prism through which the past is perceived, imagined, and recorded. That is why history remains endlessly malleable. Necessarily only a fragment of the whole, memory — with the ever-changing historical narratives that flow from it — is always vulnerable to distortion, omission, deletion, revision and clarification. For the *Altalena,* a shared consensus has yet to emerge — and probably never will — over ultimate responsibility for the tragic encounter. But because it cuts to the core of fundamental, and still unresolved, questions about political legitimacy in the Jewish state, it continues to haunt Israeli politics.

With Menachem Begin's election as Prime Minister in 1977, the *Altalena* reemerged from the depths of suppressed Israeli memory. The legitimation of the right-wing Likud (successor to the Herut party) that accompanied Begin's victory opened the floodgates, provoking debate that has continued ever since. The earliest book-length accounts, both published in Israel (in Hebrew) in 1978, reiterated partisan political arguments from thirty years earlier. Shlomo Nakdimon, a respected Israeli journalist who became Begin's media adviser, challenged claims from Ben-Gurion and his political allies that the *Altalena* was the spearhead of an Irgun *putsch*. He staunchly defended Begin, his political hero, whom he subsequently described as "like a father. You could trust him. He was honest and modest."

Nakdimon suggested that intense political friction within Ben-Gurion's government had provoked and deepened the crisis. (Indeed, the Palmach subsequently accused Ben-Gurion of creating "a military-political dictatorship" that launched a "left-wing political

'*Altalena*'" to eradicate it.) Exploiting the *Altalena* crisis to eliminate a political enemy, Nakdimon wrote, the Labor party had solidified its rule for nearly three decades. "Political motives," he concluded, "explained Ben-Gurion's actions against his rivals on the right and the left: to bring the curtain down on any actor who might threaten his exclusivity and the unique place of Mapai on Israel's political map."

But according to Uri Brenner, a Palmach commander whose *Altalena* book was published the same year, the Irgun brought the ship to Israel in blatant disregard of the ceasefire, without informing government officials. Only when it neared the coast of Israel was the government finally notified. Although Irgun representatives had agreed to turn over their military supplies, they reneged by demanding the right to unload the ship, remove the weapons to their own warehouses, and distribute them to their own units. These demands, Brenner asserted, were unacceptable to any sovereign government. Yet even Brenner concluded that the Irgun, although in "rebellion" against the absorption of its fighters into the Israel Defense Forces, was not lauching a *putsch* to overthrow the government.

Written in the afterglow of Israel's heroic struggle for independence, the early biographies of Ben-Gurion were uniformly laudatory — indeed, often fawning. To *New York Times* correspondent Gertrude Samuels, who praised him as the "Fighter of Goliaths," Ben-Gurion's life "dramatizes the rise of modern Israel and its place of moral strength in the world." In the *Altalena* crisis he displayed "an iron will," if also a "heavy heart," as he "decided for the state." Michael Bar-Zohar, who was granted privileged access to Ben-Gurion's private correspondence and state papers, described a "lion" and an "angry prophet," a true "man of war" but also an "audacious, far-sighted leader" whose "decisiveness and daring" had paved the way for the restoration of Jewish sovereignty.

Dan Kurzman, formerly a foreign correspondent for the Washington *Post*, depicted Ben-Gurion's life as "the story of Biblical prophecy." Kurzman concluded that Ben-Gurion had been determined to "fuse all fighting units into a single national army under one command" — by "whatever means" were necessary. Remaining "icily calm" during the *Altalena* crisis (disputed by his navy commander), he issued orders for the cannon fire that destroyed the ship — and, Kurzman believed, protected the government. Ben-Gurion's firm handling of the *Altalena* crisis, wrote journalist Robert St. John, "had broken a potential revolution and brought under control a terrorist organization." It was the "most brilliant" act of his political career — as long, St. John conceded, "as no one raised the philosophical and ethical question of ends and means."

In the mid-80s, following Ben-Gurion's death and the end of Begin's political career, old allegations and recriminations were recycled and revised. After Begin's term as prime minister was abruptly terminated with his resignation in 1983, amid public acrimony over the war in Lebanon, sharply critical biographers, doubtlessly reflecting dissatisfaction with his recent leadership, re-examined his responsibility for the *Altalena* crisis.

Eric Silver, a British journalist for *The Guardian*, claimed that Begin had badly misread Ben-Gurion's "motives and determination." The Irgun leader bore a share of blame for "the crossed wires and miscalculation" that brought Israel to the brink of civil war. But there was no question that the Prime Minister nurtured a "pathological hatred" of his political enemy for challenging the "divine right" of the Mapai party to rule. While ignoring an opportunity to settle his differences with Ben-Gurion without bloodshed, Silver concluded, Begin "was not planning a *putsch*."

"In this supreme test of will and force," wrote political scientist Amos Perlmutter, "Begin proved to be a terrible crisis manager," squandering an opportunity to achieve the political legitimacy that he had so long pursued. By bringing the *Altalena* to shore in violation of his pledge not to import weapons without government permission (but done with Ben-Gurion's approval), the Irgun leader had posed "a direct challenge to the authority and viability of the new Israeli government." History, Perlmutter concluded, "has vindicated Ben-Gurion."

BROTHERS AT WAR

In his study of Begin's leadership, Sasson Sofer, professor of international relations at the Hebrew University, concluded that the *Altalena* affair marked its "nadir." The Irgun leader permitted himself "to be dragged along, more than he should have, by facts and situations created by his subordinates" (a frequent complaint in Israel after Begin, as Prime Minister, yielded authority for conduct of the war in Lebanon to Defense Minister Ariel Sharon). Indeed, Sofer wrote, Begin "lost control and buckled under the pressures of the moment" by permitting *Altalena* weapons to be unloaded.

Although "a propagandist" who lacked essential attributes of leadership, Begin had nonetheless "renounced political struggle by nondemocratic means." He strongly rejected any attempt "to seize the regime," insisting that it would lead to "a bloody internal war" and the political demise of the Irgun. Far worse, it would become "catastrophic for the nation." In each instance, Sofer concedes, Begin had asserted his power to stifle potentially disruptive, indeed self-destructive, challenges to the legitimacy of the government. In the end, "the peril of civil war was a historical lesson of which Begin was deeply aware." Indeed, it was his guiding principle and he never abandoned it.

Scholars have properly located the *Altalena* crisis within the incessant internal conflict that beset the Zionist movement for nearly two decades prior to statehood. In his analysis of the birth of Israel between 1945-1949, Hebrew University professor Joseph Heller emphasized the political divisiveness that had persistently wracked the Yishuv and jeopardized its struggle for independence. The Irgun, Lehi and Palmach each pursued their own independent political — and often military — agendas. Little wonder, he concluded, that by 1948 Ben-Gurion harbored concern about an "armed coup."

In the end, Heller writes, Ben-Gurion understood the fundamental principle of leadership: "relentless consolidation of power." He was willing to accept the partition of Palestine as the best that Israel could hope for, at least in 1948. Neither the bi-nationalists on the extreme left, nor the right-wing proponents of a "greater" Israel, could overcome Ben-Gurion's insistence — framed by military and strategic realities — that partition was "the only viable option." But to achieve his goal, "the radical right" — Begin's Irgun — "had to be 'punished' and partially delegitimized."

Perceptions of Begin's challenge to the sovereignty of the state, and Ben-Gurion's justified — if belligerent — response, tended to remain constant. In her biography of Yigal Allon, Anita Shapira located the *Altalena* confrontation, "one of the most dramatic moments in state history," within "the twilight period between the Yishuv's voluntarism and a structured state authority." To Ben-Gurion, sinking the ship represented "a miraculous deliverance for the Jewish state" from the "coup d'état" that was his worst fear. "The price had indeed been terrible — Jews at war with Jews." But without paying it, Shapira believed, "the fledgling state would have toppled before it ever got on its feet."

Australian political scientist Peter Medding set the *Altalena* crisis squarely within the framework of political legitimacy. In June 1948, it was necessary for the government "to establish and institutionalize the sole and legitimate control of the use of force by constituted political authority." But the question remained whether Ben-Gurion's reliance upon force was justified. That was a more complicated issue. The Irgun, Medding suggested, was attempting "to renegotiate the terms and conditions of its participation in the state, after it had been established." With its "sovereign authority . . . under challenge," Ben-Gurion and his government utilized force "to have its authority respected." But whether legitimacy — and respect — can be secured by force remained unanswered.

Virtually the only significant challenge to the prevailing *Altalena* consensus came from maverick military historian Uri Milstein, whose scathing book *The Rabin File* was published eight months before the Prime Minister's assassination in 1995. The *Altalena*, he wrote, was a "blood libel," enabling Ben-Gurion, "in the name of democracy," to thwart "the development of a normal and liberal democracy in Israel." His determination "to eliminate, at any price, perceived threats to his authority," was vividly on display during those June days in 1948. Ben-Gurion's government, Milstein wrote, revealed "the main characteristics of Bolshevik rule — one party domination over most spheres of everyday life." The destruction of the *Altalena* enabled Ben-Gurion to "totally obliterate" any serious challenge from the political right for the next thirty years.

In the shadow of the Rabin assassination, Ehud Sprinzak published *Brother Against Brother*, his study of the Israeli "radical right," political extremism, and domestic terrorism. The governing Labor party elite, with Ben-Gurion as its leader, had long considered itself to be "the only legitimate authority." To Ben-Gurion, "a crusader for the cause of a unitary army and a single line of command," Begin's conditions for the distribution of military supplies "violated everything he believed in." As prime minister of sovereign Israel, Ben-Gurion "had both law and power on his side — there was no need for a compromise." He was determined that there would be "one center of civil and military authority" — and it would be concentrated in his hands.

During the critical weeks between the declaration of statehood and the arrival of the *Altalena*, Ben-Gurion was driven by his "personal hatred of Begin's followers and their 'terrorist mind set.'" He seized "a timely opportunity" to "teach the renegade Begin a lesson" and, in the process, to secure his own power. But Ben-Gurion's actions were "excessively ruthless": with "a touch of flexibility and compassion" he might have avoided "a great tragedy." It is "clear" that the Irgun "had no *putsch* plans."

Begin, Sprinzak acknowledged, was motivated by deep patriotism. He intended that weapons on board the *Altalena* would be used to fight against Arab invaders, not the government of Israel. Had Begin "understood Ben-Gurion's obstinacy or learned the lessons of the Season," he might have been a more flexible negotiator — even willing to surrender after the battle at Kfar Vitkin. In the end, however, Begin's restraint, Sprinzak acknowledges, "not only prevented a civil war; it established an important legacy against Jew fighting Jew" in the Jewish state.

COMPETING TRUTHS

Sprinzak's nuanced analysis of the crisis raises serious questions about Ben-Gurion's leadership that Israelis — especially on the political left — have been reluctant to confront. The *Altalena* provided the "legal excuse" (Sprinzak's apt characterization) for Ben-Gurion to destroy the political opposition that he had long detested. For better and worse, he was an authoritarian leader who demanded the consolidation of political and military power in his hands.

Begin would claim that his decision not to retaliate against his Jewish attackers was his "greatest accomplishment." Indeed, Sprinzak (despite his loyalty to the Labor party and advisory role to Rabin on domestic terrorism) praised Begin's restraint as "the most outstanding example in the modern era" of the refusal of a political leader to participate in what surely would have become "a bloody civil war." Throughout the violent crisis, Begin's bedrock principle of political honor remained unshaken: no civil war.

Ben-Gurion was relentless in his pursuit of Jewish statehood — and with it, consolidation of his own power. It may have been his greatest strength until May 14, 1948, but six weeks after independence it became his tragic flaw. He would reach his goals his way, without tolerance — indeed, with blatant contempt — for his Zionist opponents (whether on the right or left). He had mistakenly trusted that Great Britain would not abandon support for the principle of independent Jewish statehood. But in the end, rather than confront the British, Ben-Gurion targeted his despised Irgun enemy.

By now, the conflict that climaxed in the *Altalena* tragedy transcends the personalities of the political rivals who provided its *dramatis personæ*. The *Altalena* has reemerged as a contentious memory in Israel because, more than sixty years later, the issue of political legitimacy has yet to be resolved. Its legacy still haunts the Jewish state, while the terrible consequences of *sinat hinam* could yet determine its ability to survive.

Chapter 5
Memories

One year after the *Altalena* disaster, Menachem Begin's new Herut party organized a memorial ceremony. Hundreds of Irgun followers gathered on the beach not far from its burned and rusting hull, which had remained in place after the "holy cannon" destroyed it. Wreaths were dropped nearby, young sympathizers sounded a mournful dirge with drums and bugles, and prayers were recited. But Ben-Gurion — who, perhaps as a visible warning, had left the *Altalena* untouched — would not permit the ship to become a political shrine. He ordered the Israeli navy to tow it out to sea, where it was unceremoniously sunk.

Disappearing from view, the *Altalena* seemed to vanish from Zionist memory. There would be no Labor government or IDF commemoration — not then or since — of what had been claimed at the time as a resounding victory that saved the nation from internal disintegration. Rather, as Israeli scholar Asa Maron has perceptively suggested, there was "collective forgetting." The *Altalena* would receive little, if any, mention in textbooks assigned to Israeli school children. In the Haganah and Palmach museums in Tel Aviv, which properly celebrate the heroic military exploits of their brave fighting forces, the *Altalena* is all but ignored. The voluminous photography scrapbooks in the Palmach Archives contain a solitary photo of the ship that engaged its soldiers in battle. In passive language, the caption reads (in part): "An incident developed that ended in dead and wounded."

But Ben-Gurion did not forget, nor for many years would he forgive, his political enemies on the right. Indeed, as Udi Lebel has illuminated, he continued to display a vindictive determination to "delegitimize Mapai's main political rival." His government punitively denied financial benefits, extended to all other veterans of the Independence War, to wounded and disabled Irgun soldiers — even to the families of those (like Rafael Khirs) who had died fighting for their country. The government also omitted biographical information about Irgun (and Lehi) fighters from official books of reminiscences that honored Israeli war veterans. Ben-Gurion even intervened personally to have former Lehi leader Israel Eldad fired from his high school position (teaching Bible and Hebrew literature) because the Prime Minister insisted that he continued to pose a danger to the state.

In this void, Irgun sympathizers organized their own annual memorial day. Every year they posted an identical announcement: "Memorial for the Fallen of the *Altalena*: Upon [number of years] since the murder of our comrades, may God avenge them, at the hands of Cain." In the Etzel Museum, located on the Tel Aviv shore south of the battle site, the *Altalena* exhibit proudly displays the large flag of Israel that flew from the ship and was rescued just before the cannon shell destroyed it.

Four years after the *Altalena* battle, Begin and Ben-Gurion once again confronted each other, with yet another violent outcome, this time over German reparations. After the Independence War neither the United States nor Great Britain had demonstrated much interest in providing Israel with the financial assistance it so desperately needed. Indeed, Secretary of State John Foster Dulles was explicit in his determination "to improve the Moslem states' attitude toward the Western democracies" — at Israel's expense. To Ben-Gurion, West Germany seemed to offer the only possible source of financial assistance. But he was mindful of the potential for inflaming Israeli public opinion; therefore, any payments would not be defined as "compensation" for Jews murdered by the Nazis but as "restitution" for "stolen Jewish property."

News of negotiations with Germany over "blood money" instantly roiled public opinion in Israel — precisely as it had done back in 1933 when Arlosoroff negotiated the transfer agreement. Begin, whose parents and brother had been murdered in the Holocaust, was hardly alone in his fury. When Knesset debate over negotiations with Germany began in January 1952, there was sharp opposition across the political spectrum, from Herut to the Communists. Ben-Gurion vigorously defended German indemnification of Israel for Nazi war crimes against the Jewish people, insisting: "Let not the murderers of our people be also their inheritors." But a dismayed Knesset member repeated his young son's question: "What price will we get for grandpa and grandma?"

Begin delivered a fiery speech from a hotel balcony in Zion Square, just a few streets from the Knesset building. He warned: "We are prepared to suffer anything, torture chambers, concentration camps and subterranean prisons — so that any decision to deal with Germany will not happen." Still inclined in moments of crisis to histrionic oratory, he proclaimed: "When they fired on us with their cannon, I gave the order — No!" But "today I give the order — Yes!" Demanding "freedom or death," he led a crowd of hundreds to the nearby Knesset, already ringed with barbed wire and police.

Violence surged in the streets of Jerusalem. Parked cars were overturned and rocks were thrown through Knesset chamber windows. A reporter inside the building described the chaos: "the shouting of a mob not far off, the intermittent wail of police cars and ambulance sirens, sporadic explosions of gas grenades and the glow of flames from a burning car." Fumes from tear-gas used by police against the protesters penetrated the hall. When the crowd outside seemed prepared to break into the Knesset chamber, the Speaker called a recess. In the melee, dozens of policemen and civilians were injured. Ben-Gurion summoned soldiers to disperse the inflamed crowd and restore order.

After the Knesset reconvened later that afternoon, Begin assaulted the legitimacy of the government. He attacked Ben-Gurion as "a Fascist and a hooligan," a "traitor" for his willingness to do business with "the heirs of Hitler." (The Prime Minister used the identical trope for expressing his reciprocal hostility: "The first time I ever heard a speech by Begin," Ben-Gurion would write to poet Haim Gouri, "I heard the voice and ranting of Hitler.") Punctuating his tirade with biblical references, Begin appealed to Jewish pride. "You endanger our honor and independence," he railed at Ben-Gurion. "How we shall be scorned."

BROTHERS AT WAR

Begin warned Knesset members: "There are things in life that are worse than death. This is one of them. . . . There will be no negotiations with Germany. . . . There will be no reparations from Germany." The next day, in what had become a vicious war of words between mutually antagonistic political leaders with long memories, Ben-Gurion declared in a broadcast to the nation: "Yesterday, the hand of evil was raised against the sovereignty of the Parliament, and the first steps were taken to destroy democracy in Israel." He reassured the nation that "all necessary measures have been taken to safeguard democratic institutions, and law and order."

By a majority of 61-50, the Knesset gave Ben-Gurion a vote of confidence. Begin called off further demonstrations; nonetheless the Knesset approved a motion to suspend him for three months. Under the agreement reached between Israel and West Germany, the Jewish state would receive $715 million in goods and services over twelve years and Germany would pay $107 million to a committee representing world Jewish organizations. Begin never forgave the Labor government for reaching an agreement with the "murderers of the Jewish people."

It took nearly two decades for the animosity between Ben-Gurion and Begin to finally subside. Before it did, Begin once again confronted Ben-Gurion in the Knesset over the *Altalena*. Introducing a motion of no confidence in 1959, Begin asked: "What did the head of Mapai [Ben-Gurion] say? He desires 'that the young generation, that did not know Joseph, learn what happened in those days.'" Begin concurred, but changed the biblical metaphor: "The young generation that did not know Cain should learn what happened in those days."

Eight years later, when Israel confronted an imminent attack from Egypt, Syria and Jordan on its southern, northern and eastern borders, any lingering personal and political differences receded during a surge of national unity. Amid the looming crisis in May 1967, Prime Minister Levi Eshkol invited Begin to serve as Minister without Portfolio in a unity government. For the first time Begin was a member of the government, not marginalized in opposition. He suggested to Eshkol that the dire emergency required that Ben-Gurion be summoned from retirement to assume his rightful place as leader of the national unity government.

Ben-Gurion finally softened. It is recounted that when he learned of his former adversary's proposal he responded that if he had known Begin in 1948 as he did now, history might have been different. (Deference to Ben-Gurion's leadership, it seemed, remained a prerequisite for his approval.) Whenever the aging leader visited the Knesset, he asked to speak with Begin and in a 1969 note he acknowledged: "the more I have come to know you over the last years — I have come to appreciate you more."

The State of Israel has never again come as close to internecine political violence as it did during those tragic June days in 1948. But *Altalena* memories, like many repressed traumas, would continue to resurface periodically, at first on commemorative occasions, then during election campaigns and, more recently, as a weapon in newly divisive political struggles. If the sunken hull of the *Altalena* was forever out of sight, its memory was not so easily obliterated. Even as memory, the *Altalena* can still provoke acrimony and conflict.

With Begin's stunning election as Prime Minister in 1977, the gates of memory slowly opened. The story circulated in Israel, reported *New York Times* columnist William Safire, that with Begin's electoral victory anyone who sailed on the *Altalena* "is now considered equivalent to an American socialite having ancestors on the *Mayflower.*" Safire recounted the whimsical Israeli explanation for why the ship sank: "Because 200,000 people were aboard." After twenty-nine years, he concluded, the *Altalena* "has docked."

Not quite. A decade later his liberal *Times* colleague, Anthony Lewis, summoned the *Altalena* to berate Israeli settlers in the West Bank. Referring to the Irgun as a "terrorist group," Lewis approvingly cited Ben-Gurion's response to the ship that represented "an attempt to maintain a private army . . . [that] would murder the state." Now, he wrote, Israel confronted a problem "as profound and divisive as the challenge of the Altalena": the "religious-nationalist fervor" of settlers. (Lewis refrained, however, from an explicit recommendation that the government shoot them.)

Several years later, after Lewis once again invoked an *Altalena* analogy to imply an attempted coup d'état in 1948, an Irgun veteran rebuked him. According to Samuel Schachter, in a letter to the *Times*, "We did not shoot back; we did not want to ignite a civil war. We had to watch helplessly as Ben-Gurion's men shot at their imagined enemies." *Altalena* "lessons" were not as simplistic as Lewis's flawed analogies suggested.

During the 1990s, a time of unusual turbulence even for Israel — with polarizing controversy over the Oslo Accords, Prime Minister Rabin's assassination, and unremitting Palestinian terrorist attacks — the *Altalena* legacy finally began to be exhumed in its painful complexity. In 1994 Israeli documentary filmmaker Ilana Tzur produced "Altalena," a powerful blend of newsreel footage from 1948 interspersed with reflections from participants nearly fifty years later. In a Knesset screening, Tzur described the events recounted in her film as "an example of the result of blind hatred."

Distilled from memory, the *Altalena* reentered the Israeli political arena. To Knesset Speaker Shevah Weiss, there were lessons to be learned "about testing the limits of obedience to orders." Whoever challenges the authority of the Knesset, he asserted, "only sows the seed of civil war." Dov Shilansky, a fighter on board the *Altalena* (and only recently Speaker of the Knesset) who had organized the screening, identified the dilemma: "Do you obey an order like that and then afterwards say you were ashamed of your part or do you refuse it and tell your grandchildren the reason you were sent to prison?" He "would not lift a finger against a Jewish soldier." But Arik Nehamkin, a commander of military operations against the *Altalena*, responded: "I would do it again today. In the army, one must obey orders."

Tzur's interviews with Irgun, Haganah and Palmach veterans revealed enduring anguish among soldiers on both sides of the conflict. They summoned long buried and still deeply troubling experiences as young fighters for Jewish independence who were commanded to attack, or were targeted by, their Jewish "brothers." For some, the responsibility of the government of a sovereign nation to protect itself against challenges from independent military groups remained paramount. Yitzhak Rabin, by then Prime Minister, still defended Ben-Gurion's orders — and, implicitly, his own obedience — as necessary to suppress a "*putsch.*"

After Rabin signed the Oslo Accords with Yasir Arafat, his role as Palmach officer on the beach during the *Altalena* battle subjected him to renewed vituperation in right-wing circles. Yigal Amir, his assassin, referred to Rabin as "the *Altalena* murderer." Moshe Feiglin, the founding leader of the pro-settlement organization *Zo Artzeinu* ("This is our land"), claimed that there was "no difference" between Baruch Goldstein, who had recently killed 29 Muslims in prayer in the Cave of the Patriarchs in Hebron, and Rabin, who "murdered" 16 Jews from the *Altalena*. A pamphlet distributed to Knesset members cited "all [Rabin's] sins from the *Altalena* to the treacherous act of Oslo."

It took fifty years after the event before a monument to the *Altalena* was placed on Bograshov beach in Tel Aviv, near the site of the battle. The inscription offered a spare, and curious, summary of what had transpired there:

> On 14 Sivan 5708, 21.6.1948, in coordination with the government's representatives, the ship Altalena arrived at the coast of the homeland with 930 IZL fighters on board. Most of them were Holocaust survivors who had come to join the IDF in the war against the Arab invader. The ship contained large quantities of weapons and ammunition. Due to disagreements between the government of Israel and the IZL headquarters in regard to the allocation of a small part of the weapons to the IZL battalion in Jerusalem, which was not yet part of the territory of the State of Israel (the Haganah, the IZL and LEHI still operated there independently), the ship was shelled at this shore upon the orders of the provisional government.

Below this summary, in parallel columns, were carved the names of sixteen Irgun fighters "who fell in the tragic event": Michael Victor

BROTHERS AT WAR

Asoid, Eliezer Weitz, Isaac Cohen, Daniel Levy, David Mitrani, Abraham Oded, Mendel Kaufman, Shlomo Kotnovsky, Aryeh Victor Pakula, Abraham Cohen, Aaron Karsenti, Itamar Lifshitz, Avraham Stavsky, Dan Glickman, Dov Kelner, Zvi Reifer.

The first three sentences succinctly presented basic factual information: date of arrival; number of passengers; and contents of the cargo. But the lengthy concluding sentence, comprising nearly half the inscription, raised still vexing questions. Why did "coordination" become "disagreement," climaxing in violence? Who were the unnamed people in the government and Irgun "headquarters" whose failure to agree had precipitated the clash? Why did a "small" allocation of weapons become such a menacing provocation to the government? What boundaries defined the State of Israel? Even fifty years later there still were no conclusive answers.

After the turn of the century some Israeli politicians began to grapple, if unsteadily, with the legacy of the *Altalena*. Prime Minister Ariel Sharon, speaking each year between 2001-3 at annual memorial observances, condemned the "groundless hatred" that led to the tragedy and praised Begin for his steadfast insistence: "civil war — never." But in 2004, at a memorial service for Ben-Gurion at Sde Boker, Sharon underscored the obligation, under the rule of law, to accept the decisions of legitimate government authorities.

On both sides of the political divide, the meaning of the *Altalena* remained bitterly contested. Knesset member Moshe Arens, former Minister of Defense in the Begin and Netanyahu governments, was outraged (in 2001) when Ben-Gurion's order to sink the *Altalena* was suggested as the solution to Yasir Arafat's internal conflict with Hamas. Ben-Gurion's attempt "to liquidate his opponents," Arens wrote in *Haaretz*, marked "a tragic chapter in Israel's history. . . . Associating it with Arafat's current predicament is inexcusable."

But as Palestinian terrorism in Israel continued unabated during the second intifada (while Arafat, behind the scenes, actively encouraged it) the Israeli left popularized the Arafat-*Altalena* analogy. Uri Avnery, a maverick peace activist who had joined the

Irgun in his teens, praised Ben-Gurion for ending, "once and for all, the existence of private armies in Israel." But no Palestinian "sacred cannon," he advised, should be fired until statehood had been achieved. Only then, as in 1948, would such a confrontation with armed militants be justified.

The call for a Palestinian *"Altalena"* (with the implication that the Irgun and Hamas were identical) stirred passionate debate. Hebrew University professor Moshe Maoz, a 13-year-old Irgun member in 1948 (who recalled that his heart was broken when the *Altalena* was destroyed), had come to realize that "no modern state can function unless its armed forces are under one central authority." But Maoz (who had served as Ben-Gurion's adviser on Arab issues) rejected the wisdom of an *Altalena* reprise merely to shore up the Palestinian Authority. Israel, he wrote, "should hasten the day when Abu Mazen [Arafat] will be ready for his own *Altalena* moment" — presumably, following the Israeli model, once the Palestinians had their own state.

Altalena analogies erupted in the Knesset when Justice Minister Yosef Lapid from the left-wing Shinui party compared Palestinian Prime Minister Abbas's dilemma over terrorism to Ben-Gurion's confrontation with the Irgun. Sharply rebuked by a Likud colleague, Lapid denied any intention to equate the Irgun with Arab terrorists. He was chastised for his "folly" by journalist Uri Dan, who seized the opportunity to blame "forgers of history" teaching in Israeli universities for linking the *Altalena* to Palestinian terrorist groups.

The Arafat-*Altalena* analogy quickly caught on as a teachable moment. A Palestinian Authority official told the *Jerusalem Post* that in confronting Hamas and Islamic Jihad, "we have to act like Ben-Gurion in 1948." *New York Times* columnist Thomas Friedman (politically aligned with the Israeli left since his undergraduate years at Brandeis) also suggested that Arafat needed his *"Altalena* moment."

Not long after proposals for a Palestinian *"Altalena"* had receded, a far more volatile analogy emerged. Prime Minister Sharon's decision to remove 9,000 Jewish settlers from Gaza provoked acrimonious debate throughout the nation over the future of Jewish settlements. It stirred *Altalena* memories that had been simmering ever since the first settlements were built after the Six-Day War.

When the Elon Moreh settlement was established over government objections in 1974, soldiers had been dispatched to remove settlers, by force if necessary. As Rabbi Tzvi Yehuda Kook, the inspirational mentor of the nascent settlement movement, stood resolutely with the settlers it seemed to leader Benny Katzover that their venerated rabbi was "standing on the *Altalena*." Reflecting on the encounter, which resulted in the removal and arrest of disobedient settlers, poet Haim Gouri wrote in *Davar* that it "takes us back to the very beginning of the state, to the dispute we thought was over. . . ." To journalist Gershom Gorenberg, writing a sharply critical history of the origins of the settlement movement, it was evident that Gouri had detected "a whiff of a sea breeze carrying smoke from the *Altalena*."

One year later, when settlers refused to leave a site in nearby Sabastia, Prime Minister Rabin was prepared to send in the army — as Ben-Gurion, his political commander, had done in 1948. But military chief of staff Mordechai Gur, anticipating the need for as many as 5000 soldiers to expel the settlers, hesitated. Rabin was furious. His rage, Gorenberg concluded, was understandable, for Gur "was avoiding the order that Yitzhak Rabin had accepted and carried out" during the *Altalena* confrontation: "to establish that there was a state, that there was one government, even if establishing this fact required fighting other Jews." Noting that Rabin had not replaced Gur with a more compliant officer, Gorenberg wrote: "Here is the tragedy of Yitzhak Rabin: for the second time in his life he faced the *Altalena* test, and unlike the first time, he failed it."

This harsh judgment (published in 2006, a flourishing time of *Altalena* analogies sparked by the Gaza settlement evacuations) exposed Gorenberg's political preferences. He made it clear that he despised "religious radicals, convinced they were fulfilling God's plan for history." He believed that settlement (at least by religious Zionists) had "led to the state's gradual unraveling, . . . undercutting its authority." It was little wonder that Gorenberg found an *Altalena* reprise so appealing. By then, it had become a favorite left-wing trope, revealing the loathing of secular Israelis for religious settlers who claimed the biblical homeland as integral — both geographically and spiritually — to the Jewish state.

Opening the winter session of the Knesset in 2004, Speaker Reuven Rivlin compared the besieged Gaza settlers, facing expulsion by their own government, to Irgun members when the Haganah betrayed them to the British and Ben-Gurion ordered the attack on their ship. Rivlin warned against yet another national tragedy that would result from the delegitimization of settlers, who comprised "the most pioneering, Zionist and dedicated group" of Israelis. Responding to Rivlin, poet Haim Hefer recalled his own participation in the defense of Palmach headquarters from an anticipated Irgun assault during the *Altalena* crisis: "I understood that this is how a *putsch* is carried out."

Rivlin countered: "It was not a *putsch*. It was a shame for the Jewish people" that demonstrated "foolishness or malice" by Israeli political leaders. Civil war had been averted "thanks to one man ... who placed the unity of the nation above his own life and the life of his fighters, Menachem Begin." Knesset member Avshalom Vilan from the left-wing Meretz party surely had the *Altalena* in mind when he told *Haaretz*: "we must fight extremist settlers by all possible means... if need be we'll open fire ... we'll shoot to hit ... the sovereign authority must announce that in order to preserve itself it too is ready to kill."

As the *Altalena* resurfaced from repressed memory into contemporary Israeli political scuffles, journalist Yaron London observed that it "continues to glow like coals." For the government to exercise its "sovereign duty," London wrote in *Yediot Aharonot*, it must once again use "muscles" against those who violently opposed its decisions. And if an Israeli *Altalena* reprise proved insufficient, he also favored a "Palestinian *Altalena*" to secure the unified political authority that might hasten peace with Israel.

The Israeli press, which enthusiastically supported the Gaza expulsion, vigorously defended Ben-Gurion's action as a model to emulate. In an article entitled "We Are Not Afraid," *Haaretz* journalist Yoel Marcus affirmed the vital lesson from 1948: "sinking the *Altalena* established the principle of one army and one authority" under unitary sovereignty. In "Our *Altalena* and Theirs," Ido Aviana wrote in *De'Ot* that Ben-Gurion's display of "determined military action" in 1948 provided the precedent for current confrontations with militant groups (whether Israeli or Palestinian) that "seek to undermine the legitimacy" of government authority.

Moshe Negbi, legal commentator for the Israel Broadcasting Authority, complained (in *Haaretz*) that "Ben-Gurion's successors have demonstrated total limpness in imposing law and order on extremists.... It is this limpness that has brought down upon us the malignancy of the Jewish settlements" and their "fanatics." Negbi asserted "the right — and the duty — of democracy to defend itself and suppress statements and demonstrations whose aim is . . . to thwart the majority's abilities to carry out its policies." On the political left, Ben-Gurion remained an inspirational model; he certainly could not be accused of "limpness."

Historian Yosef Salmon warned that "the integrity of Israeli society and its government" was under attack from those who promised to obstruct the disengagement from Gaza. He compared the prospect of settler resistance to the *Altalena* confrontation, Ben-Gurion's disbanding of the Palmach, and the German reparations controversy — when "the state exercised its power and authority over minorities that threatened its legitimate right to maintain control." Now as then, "the justification for majority rule" — and, implicitly, for the use of force to defend it — "was clear to all." Like the Irgun in 1948, Salmon warned, a new religious Zionist elite "believe[s] themselves to be the people, the nation, the raison d'être of the Jewish state."

The flurry of encouragement for another *Altalena* roused Shmuel Katz, who had been a member of the Irgun high command in 1948 and then a founder of the Herut party, a Knesset member, and Jabotinsky's biographer. Ninety-one years old in 2005, he fiercely defended Begin and the Irgun. Katz castigated those who warned that Israel was on the road to civil war over the Gaza disengagement, predicting (inaccurately, as it turned out) that if Prime Minister Sharon persisted with the Gaza expulsion, he would confront his own "*Altalena*." These "pundits," he wrote in the *Jerusalem Post*, were "conjuring up the *Altalena* myth of a revolt that was never planned and never took place, a fiction woven by an unscrupulous politician at the cost of a score of innocent young lives and the loss of a valuable ship and an invaluable store of arms."

Recounting his version of the *Altalena* tragedy to a new generation of Israelis, Katz berated Ben-Gurion for claiming that there was no advance notice until the day before the ship arrived at Kfar Vitkin, nor had permission for its landing been requested. "Every word of this story," Katz wrote, "was false." "The memory of the *Altalena*," he claimed, "is being manipulated for political purposes to facilitate the expulsion of the Jews from Gush Katif [Gaza]."

Despite dire warnings of violent confrontations, the Gaza evacuation proved largely peaceful, if nonetheless traumatic for Israelis who had settled there, some for nearly forty years, with the encouragement of their government. Now it was forcing them to abandon their homes, fields, greenhouses, and synagogues — all of which euphoric Palestinians triumphantly destroyed after their departure. With the Gaza expulsion, conflict over the future of all Jewish settlements — and a proliferation of *Altalena* analogies — loomed ominously on the Israeli political horizon.

During Knesset debate in 2005 over the expulsion of Orthodox settlers from Yitzhar, Prime Minister Sharon was accused of wanting "a second *Altalena*" so that he, too, could "fire the 'holy cannon.'" He was sharply rebuked by settler groups: "You will not get a second *Altalena* from us. You will not get a civil war from us, because we — the citizens whom you wish to go to war against — will not fight against our brothers." A Knesset member from the Labor Party, citing the *Altalena* as a model for government action, was criticized for "terrible rhetoric [that was] a call to murder citizens, for bloodshed."

BROTHERS AT WAR

As national debate over settlements became increasingly acrimonious, some stanch supporters urged soldiers to refuse to obey orders to evacuate settlers. They cited the precedent of Palmach soldiers who had disobeyed orders to fire on the *Altalena*: "Refuse to obey the transfer order against your brothers, just as . . . soldiers refused to shoot at their brothers in Ben-Gurion's day." A new group called "A Mother's Voice," proposing "to disengage the Israel Defense Forces from the disengagement," held its founding conference on the beach where the attack against the *Altalena* had occurred. One of its founders, former Palmach soldier Yael Sherez Polkovsky, publicly expressed her regret that she had not disobeyed orders to fire on the ship. Recalling the war between brothers in 1948, 82-year-old Yosef Nachmias, then a company commander on board the *Altalena*, recounted the refusal of his own brother, a Palmach fighter, to shoot at the ship because he knew that his sibling was on board. For him, killing brothers was not merely a metaphor.

On the 59th anniversary of the *Altalena* battle, one hundred Israelis boarded the *Sababa* in Haifa port to sail to the spot where the ship sank. Irgun veterans were joined by a contingent of new Russian immigrants who had discovered in the *Altalena* story a way to strengthen their own Israeli identity. As a Russian participant cast a wreath of daisies into the water, another declared: "This is a memorial to our brethren who were butchered by Cain." Journalist Lily Galili, who described the commemoration ceremony in *Haaretz*, noted: "The state is almost 60 years old, and it is still about Cain and Abel."

Several days later, at a commemorative gathering at the Etzel Museum, Yosef Nachmias told the audience: "My heart is still bleeding. The hate has gone down, but the wound has not healed." Russian immigrant sympathizers with the Irgun, he claimed, were revitalizing Zionism at a time when its roots had withered. Dr. Mark Radotzky, who had arrived in Israel from Tashkent seventeen years earlier, had first heard about the *Altalena* following the Rabin assassination. Only then did he learn of the slain prime minister's role in the attack. It had "defined which political side I would take here. . . . If I were looking for the brotherhood of nations, I would have stayed in Tashkent. [But] I came to live in a Jewish state." On board the *Altalena,* he believed, "not only people were killed, so was the Israeli democracy. . . . We have come to rebuild it."

Altalena memories resurfaced yet again during acrimonious debate over military disobedience. After a ceremony at the Western Wall in October 2009, two religious soldiers who displayed a sign protesting settler expulsions served time in jail for their misbehavior. One of them, Aryeh Arbus, a soldier-student in the *hesder* program (enabling religious soldiers to combine military service and Torah study), was discharged from the army after refusing to express regret for his action. Then two *hesder* soldiers who displayed a banner from the roof of their military base opposing expulsion were sentenced to thirty days in jail, demoted in rank, and dismissed from command and combat duties.

These confrontations widened the secular-religious chasm. Rabbi Eliezer Melamed, head of the Har Bracha yeshiva where the soldiers studied, supported disobedience in response to military orders to expel Jews from their homes. Rabbi Gur Galon, a teacher there, referred to a rabbinical edict, issued fifteen years earlier, prohibiting the evacuation of Jewish settlements. Former Chief Rabbi Avraham Shapira insisted that settlement evacuation "contradicts our holy Torah faith." At a Bar-Ilan University conference on insubordination, Rabbi Elyakim Levanon, head of the yeshiva in the settlement of Elon Moreh, declared his support for the refusal to obey military orders under certain circumstances. "Insubordination is a lethal and destructive act," Rabbi Levanon conceded, "but there are instances when we use chemotherapy and radiation to stop a cancerous growth."

More moderate religious leaders, rejecting the applicability of Jewish law (*halacha*) to matters of state, opposed military disobedience. According to the venerable rabbinical principle of *dina demalkhuta dina,* the law of the state is the law that must be obeyed.

Warning that theologicans should not claim to be political experts, they cautioned against the delegitimization of the state or its army.

Defense Minister (and former Prime Minister) Ehud Barak, whose tolerance for religious settlers — no less for disobedient religious soldiers — was conspicuously lacking, retaliated by removing the Har Bracha yeshiva from the *hesder* program. His action, yeshiva students complained, caused a split in "the sacred partnership between the IDF and the national religious community that has existed practically since the state was founded."

But Yehuda Ben Meir, former Deputy Minister of Foreign Affairs in the Begin government, praised Barak's decision. Expulsion, he claimed, sent a necessary message to the religious nationalist community that "the government has decided to stop accepting, compromising and bowing to the nationalist-religious extremists and is drawing a line in the sand at the refusal to serve in the IDF." Condemning the "brazen political protest" of religious soldiers, he warned that they "are likely to become a strategic threat to both the unity of the IDF and the future of the State of Israel."

Amid this political embroglio over settlers and soldiers, *Altalena* analogies proliferated. Writing in *Haaretz*, Hebrew University political scientist Shlomo Avineri accused settlement defenders of attempting to undermine the "historic achievement of Zionism," the creation of "a single binding [national] authority" for the Jewish state. Ben-Gurion's decision to attack the *Altalena*, he conceded, may have displayed "ruthless determination," but it assured to the Israel Defense Forces "a monopoly on the legitimate use of force." The pain and distress of settlement supporters was understandable, Avineri acknowledged, but "in the Jewish state only one legitimate body is authorized to enforce political decisions."

When six infantry soldiers refused to participate in the demolition of new structures in the settlement outpost of Negohot, Prime Minister Benjamin Netanyahu — sounding very much like Ben-Gurion in 1948 — asserted ominously: "If you support this refusal, it will bring about the collapse of the state." It may seem farfetched to suggest that the refusal of a few religious soldiers to participate in the destruction of a settlement outpost constituted a mortal danger to Israel. To Defense Minister Barak, however, Israeli leaders were confronting "the same fateful decision that David Ben-Gurion faced in the first days of the state." Ben-Gurion knew "how to act decisively and without compromise to guarantee that the IDF and all its soldiers and commanders would be under the sole authority of the elected government." Barak, like the prime minister whose memory he revered, demanded obedience to orders.

Yet the refusal to serve in the Israel Defense Forces, or to obey orders from its officers, was hardly novel. Back in 1982, during the war in Lebanon (while Menachem Begin was Prime Minister), 3000 reservists had proclaimed their unwillingness to serve. For their disobedience some were court-martialed; others were sent to military prison. From their opposition emerged *Yesh Gvul* ("there is a limit"), an organization dedicated to defending soldiers "who refuse duties of a repressive or aggressive nature." Although some leaders on the political left opposed the new organization, they had not advocated harsh punitive action by the government against disobedient soldiers. Nor did *Altalena* analogies, with their implicit demand to violently repress challenges to national authority, swirl through Israel. Indeed, the (right-wing) government was vilified for waging an unpopular war.

Twenty years later, fifty-one reserve soldiers and officers who refused to fight beyond the provisional pre-1967 borders of Israel formed a new organization based on the principle that "Refusal to serve in the Territories is Zionism." Then, in 2003, more than two-dozen air force pilots — most of whom were no longer on active duty — published a letter indicating, in principle, their refusal to participate in "illegal and immoral" actions that were "a direct result of the ongoing occupation" of the West Bank. (Pilots on active duty were suspended.) When secular soldiers declined to serve in wars whose morality they challenged, the Israeli left had no problem with disobedience. It did not castigate them with *Altalena* reminders. The double standard was palpable: what had been permissible (for secular soldiers) ever since the Lebanon war was now forbidden (to religious soldiers).

So the problem of legitimacy that had once roiled Israeli politics, climaxing with the attack on the *Altalena*, has continued to torment the Jewish state. In 1948 the struggle was between left and right. Now, amid sharp disagreement over where final national borders should be drawn (with or without the settlements where 300,000 Israelis now live), there are competing religious and secular definitions of Jewish statehood, obligations of citizenship, and even legal authority. Until this legitimacy conundrum is resolved — if it ever is — the *Altalena* is likely to continue to haunt Israeli society.

Epilogue

Should Israel and the Palestinian Authority ever reach agreement on the terms of peace, their implementation is likely to require the forcible removal of tens of thousands of Jewish settlers from their homes. But few Israelis on the left, who argue passionately for this outcome, are likely to recognize the similarity between soldiers who would refuse to obey orders to evict settlers and the Haganah and Palmach soldiers — and *Altalena* fighters — who refused to attack their Jewish "brothers" in 1948.

Such a confrontation, if it comes, will once again expose Israel's unresolved identity struggle: Jewish state, secular state, democratic state, democratic Jewish state, state of the Jewish people? It has the ominous potential for violence on a scale that would reduce the *Altalena* to historical insignificance by comparison. There can be no disagreement with the claim that national sovereignty requires the concentration of political authority in a duly elected government. But ever since 1948, Israelis have faced the tormenting question of whether every government action — even the application of excessive force against its own people for political purposes — is legitimate. When do violent means, tainted by partisanship, undercut legitimate ends?

At a crucial moment, confronting the urgent necessity to protect the state and defend its sovereignty, did David Ben-Gurion decide wisely when he issued the command to attack fellow Jews? In his unrelenting determination to concentrate authority in his hands, did he undermine, rather than strengthen, legitimacy in the new nation? Did he set a dangerous precedent for battles between Jewish brothers that has haunted Israel ever since — and may yet, if the government threatens settlers with expulsion from their homes, explode into a far more volatile internecine conflagration than anything that happened in 1948?

BROTHERS AT WAR

Lingering reverberations from the *Altalena* continue to spark acrimony in Israel. This disagreement is not likely to end in the foreseeable future — but only to be recast in different settings. Ever since Ben-Gurion read the Proclamation of Independence on that historic day in May 1948, Israel has harbored internal contradictions that could yet plunge its people into the most devastating war imaginable: civil war. Jewish history, after all, hardly negates that possibility.

As an admiring student of American history, Ben-Gurion was determined that a Jewish state would follow its democratic path. He had arrived in the United States for the first time in 1915 to rally support for the nascent Zionist cause. Thereafter, he subsequently wrote, he "always dreamed of America" as a model for the aspiring Jewish state: "We who want to build a new country in the desert, to raise our ruins, we must see how exiles, persecuted in England, constructed a state so rich, with unequaled power." Ben-Gurion remained convinced of the fundamental compatibility between the United States and Israel. Both nations were "linked to a democratic system of government, based on liberty, government freely elected by the people, freedom of thought, freedom of speech, freedom of debate."

Yet despite his avid interest in American history, and his evident admiration for American principles of freedom, it is unlikely that Ben-Gurion would have been familiar with President George Washington's response to the Whiskey Rebellion, early in the life of the new American nation. But the *Altalena* confrontation, in uncanny ways, had an American antecedent.

In 1791, two years after the ratification of the Constitution, a Congressional tax on alcohol provoked vehement protests from farmers in western Pennsylvania whose grain harvests would incur the levy. A federal tax collector was tarred and feathered and several hundred men surrounded the house of a federal marshal, whose arrest they demanded. Federalist government officials in Philadelphia (where the American capital was then located) were stunned by what they perceived to be a menacing internal challenge to the new

EPILOGUE

nation. Treasury Secretary Alexander Hamilton, who had proposed the whiskey tax, was eager to assert national authority to suppress what he feared was an incipient rebellion. But President Washington, more restrained, merely issued a proclamation condemning the farmers' challenge to authority and threatening to enforce the whiskey tax.

Pennsylvania farmers, infuriated and ever more attentive to revolutionary developments in France, raised their own flag of rebellion. They set up mock guillotines and extralegal courts, even threatening to seize weapons from a federal arsenal in Pittsburgh. Attorney General William Bradford described "a well formed and regular plan for weakening and perhaps overthrowing the General Government." A federal judge certified that western Pennsylvania was in a state of rebellion. Washington issued another proclamation, indicating his intention to call upon the militia to suppress the tax revolt. Reluctant to use force to dispel the protesters, he was nonetheless determined to assert government authority — and, as the first president of the new nation, his own. Before taking any action, however, he dispatched a peace commission to meet with the rebels to demand that they renounce violence or face prosecution.

When it finally became evident, by 1794, that negotiations had failed, Washington summoned a militia of nearly 13,000 men — a larger number than he had often commanded during the Revolutionary War. His conscription order sparked violent protests in eastern Virginia and Maryland, where some men evaded the command to report for duty. When the federal militia finally arrived in Carlisle, violence once again erupted. Three civilians, including an unarmed boy, were killed before the rebellion was quashed.

Twenty whiskey rebels were arrested and brought to Philadelphia for trial. Most were released or acquitted; two were convicted of treason and sentenced to death by hanging. Washington pardoned them. The challenge to government authority had been squelched; national supremacy was successfully asserted (and with it, presidential and Federalist party power). The Whiskey Rebellion, although quickly forgotten, was the most menacing episode of armed resistance to the authority of the American government until cannons at Fort Sumter ignited the Civil War.

Ben-Gurion might have learned from the response to the Whiskey Rebellion of the first president of the young American republic. To be sure, the United States no longer was at war in 1791, confronting invading armies at its borders as Israel did in June 1948. But with a month-long United Nations ceasefire in place when the *Altalena* arrived, Ben-Gurion had time and space for at least attempting to negotiate an agreement — as Washington did — before war with Arab states resumed. Instead, issuing a ten-minute ultimatum, he ordered a military attack.

To ask an irresistible counter-factual question: What might Ben-Gurion have done differently? How might an alternative Israeli scenario have played out, especially given Israel's urgent need — as he had informed his government immediately after independence was declared — for weapons and munitions? Rather than issuing his ultimatum at Kfar Vitkin, Ben-Gurion might have authorized the resumption of negotiations with Begin. The government had already agreed that 20 percent of the weapons on board the *Altalena* would go to Irgun forces in Jerusalem. There is no reason to believe that Begin, having already instructed the ship to delay its arrival in Israel until the government gave permission for it to land, would have refused to discuss additional weapons distributions.

Indeed, Begin sailed on board the *Altalena* from Kfar Vitkin to Tel Aviv with the expressed hope — futile though it proved to be — of negotiating with the government. He wanted recognition for the Irgun contribution to the war for Jewish independence, not a Jewish civil war. It can never be known, of course, whether the weapons and munitions from the *Altalena*, had they reached Irgun fighters in Jerusalem as promised, could have reversed the loss of the Old City to the Arab Legion.

Ben-Gurion met with his military advisers early in the morning of the *Altalena*'s arrival in Tel Aviv. He might have considered, and even accepted, the recommendations of his own navy commander for ways to immobilize the ship without resorting to deadly force.

EPILOGUE

But the agitated prime minister seized the opportunity to retaliate against his political nemesis. The leader of the Yishuv who had not confronted British authorities over their despicable treatment of desperate Holocaust refugees on board the *Exodus* now displayed his eagerness, as Prime Minister, to order soldiers into battle against a ship with his Jewish enemies on board.

Had Ben-Gurion even minimally displayed Washington's attributes — patience rather than fury, the application of limited force only as a last resort, and forgiveness rather than vindictiveness — an Israeli tragedy and trauma might have been averted. But that was not Ben-Gurion's way. Indeed, it is tempting to wonder whether he projected upon his Irgun foe precisely the intention to resort to force that he himself harbored — and acted upon (while Begin, who would never command his fighters to shoot at Jews, may have imagined that Ben-Gurion was bound by the same constraint). Who — Ben-Gurion or Begin — better understood that even a worthy end might not justify the violent means necessary to attain it?

By 1948 there was a toxic legacy of political bitterness and recrimination between the Zionist left and right. The conviction of Avraham Stavsky for the Arlosoroff murder, and his death on board the *Altalena*, bracketed fifteen years of internecine acrimony, discord, and even violence. When a crisis loomed during a crucial period in the decisive struggle for Jewish statehood, Ben-Gurion was hardly inclined to tolerate political challenges, whether real or imagined.

Ben-Gurion did not — then or subsequently — present even a scintilla of evidence to justify his claim, reiterated by loyal followers, that Begin and the Irgun were preparing a *putsch* to overthrow the government. If, indeed, there was such evidence, Begin certainly should have been arrested and brought to trial for treason. In reality, however, Begin's only political offense had been to challenge Ben-Gurion's authority. Had Begin intended more, surely Ben-Gurion would not have permitted him to lead his Herut Party into the first Israeli election, nor become its leader in the Knesset.

BROTHERS AT WAR

Once the *Altalena* crisis loomed, Begin — who had been so relentlessly vilified and hunted during the Season — had reason to anticipate a forceful response from his political nemesis. But even after the Kfar Vitkin attack, he badly misread Ben-Gurion's intentions and resolve. Certainly, he miscalculated the prospects for reaching an agreement with Ben-Gurion once the *Altalena* arrived in Tel Aviv. The Prime Minister was hardly inclined to honor his political rival with recognition and respect, which Begin may have craved too much.

Ben-Gurion would exercise the force necessary to secure his own political domination at a precarious transitional moment, during a war for survival, when the new state had little more than an embryonic government. Only weeks before independence was declared he had been appointed (by an interparty committee) Chairman of the Provisional Zionist Council to preside over the interim legislature. National elections were still many months away. In this fraught transitional moment the *Altalena* tragedy was triggered by his aggressive, unyielding determination to use military force to strengthen the claim of his government to legitimacy. It remains an ineradicable stain on his legacy as the heroic leader of the struggle for Jewish independence who then guided the young state as its prime minister for thirteen years.

By 1967 the internecine rivalries that had tormented the Yishuv during the British Mandatory era and shaken Israel at its birth had finally receded. Disappearing into a memory hole, they were an embarrassing, if not unsavory, episode of Zionist history that was barely recalled and rarely scrutinized. There was not another hunting season. The "holy cannon" that destroyed the *Altalena* was not fired again.

That June, in a stunningly successful preemptive military strike, the Israeli air force destroyed 350 Egyptian planes, effectively ending what became known as the Six-Day War early in the morning of the first day. The euphoric return of Jews to their most ancient holy sites — the Western Wall in Jerusalem, the tombs of the biblical patriarchs and matriarchs in Hebron, Rachel's tomb outside

EPILOGUE

Bethlehem — healed, at least for an ecstatic historical moment shared by virtually the entire nation, the polarized political divisions that had beset Israel even before, and ever since, its founding.

Then, in 1976, after terrorists from the Popular Front for the Liberation of Palestine hijacked an Air France plane flying from Tel Aviv to Paris with 300 passengers, the Israel Defense Forces flew elite commandos one thousand miles to Entebbe in Uganda to execute a brilliant rescue operation. Five years later, a surprise Israeli air attack — authorized by Prime Minister Begin — destroyed the Iraqi nuclear reactor at Osirak. These stunning displays of airborne military prowess exemplified the determination of Israel to protect its citizens and assure its survival. They also demonstrated how far the Jewish state had come since its fate had turned on the ability of rickety ships to bring desperate refugees and urgently needed weapons to its shores.

If the past can be remembered, forgotten, or invented, it can also be subverted. In their own inversion of history, Palestinian Arabs have appropriated Jewish and Zionist memory to claim the biblical Land of Israel as their own. A people without an identifiable national history before the early 20th century has mimicked Jewish and Zionist history to create their own illusory past.

Relying on the Hebrew Bible, Palestinian Arabs claim Ishmael, Abraham's son born to his servant Hagar, as their ancient ancestor, while citing the Canaanites, displaced (according to the biblical narrative) by the Israelite conquest, as their forebears. Rejecting irrefutable historical and archeological evidence, they deny that Jews ever had a Temple in Jerusalem or that the Western Wall has been a Jewish holy place ever since its destruction. Yet triumphalist Islam chose to build its hallowed Dome of the Rock and Al-Aksa mosque on that very site — precisely because it was a Jewish holy place. So, too, Muslims seized the Cave of the Patriachs in Hebron, where Jews had worshipped long before the birth of Islam, and barred them from entry for seven hundred years. Now, inventing a past they never had, Palestinians dispatch flotillas of ships, modeled on the journey of the *Exodus*, to defame Israel in the court of world opinion. Even the *Altalena*, the battle of Jewish brothers, serves their cause.

Rabbi Abraham Yitzhak haCohen Kook, the chief rabbi of Mandatory Palestine, pondered the tragedy of 1st century Jerusalem. He taught that the Temple, destroyed by *sinat hinam*, could only be rebuilt with *ahavat hinam*, "groundless love." But neither his teaching, nor his preferred fusion of religious Orthodoxy and Zionist nationalism, took hold in the young Zionist state. Instead, Israel was born amid the groundless hatred that was tragically on display during the two-day war of brothers (*milchemet achim*) in June 1948. It still confronts the ominous possibility of a recurrence, this time between secular and religious Zionists.

The *Altalena* episode, and the killing of Jews by Jews that accompanied it, remains a lingering, self-inflicted wound from Israel's heroic struggle for independence. If wisely used as historical memory, the *Altalena* might serve Israelis as a reminder of the ominous possibility that civil war could destroy Jewish national sovereignty. If not, *Altalena* memories may finally — and disastrously — be erased by an even more devastating tragedy.

Those who now yearn for a reprise of the *Altalena* should beware of what they wish for; they may get it. The citizens and government of the State of Israel must choose between gratuitous hatred and groundless love. The future of their nation is likely to turn on their fateful choice.

Bibliographical Note

The following archival collections were consulted: Central Zionist Archives and Menachem Begin Heritage Center Archives (Jerusalem); Jabotinsky Institute Archives, Etzel Museum, Beit Ha-Palmach Archives and Haganah Archives (Tel Aviv); and David Ben-Gurion Archives (Sde Boker).

Introduction

For Max Weber on legitimacy, see "Politics as a Vocation," in H.H. Gerth and C. Wright Mills (eds.), *From Max Weber: Essays in Sociology* (New York, 1958), 78. For Bernard Lewis, see *Faith and Power: Religion and Politics in the Middle East* (New York, 2010), 142. The fearful reluctance of American Jewish leaders and "the President's Jews" to speak out during the Nazi era is explored in Gulie Ne'eman Arad, *America, Its Jews, and the Rise of Nazism* (Bloomington, 2000), chs. 6-8. For rescue efforts: Tuvia Friling, *Arrows in the Dark: David Ben-Gurion, the Yishuv Leadership, and Rescue Attempts During the Holocaust* (Madison, 2005).

Chapter 1. Groundless Hatred

The classic, and enduringly vivid, English language edition of Josephus is *The Wars of the Jews; or, the History of the Destruction of Jerusalem* in *The Works of Flavius Josephus*, Tr. William Wriston (London, 1871). The best modern analysis is Martin Goodman, *Rome and Jerusalem: The Clash of Ancient Civilizations* (New York, 2007). For historiographical insight: James S. McLaren, *Turbulent Times? Josephus and Scholarship on Judaea in the First Century CE* (Sheffield, 1998). Also helpful were Goodman, *The Ruling Class of Judaea* (Cambridge, 1987); Tessa Rajak, *Josephus: The Historian and His Society* (London, 1983); Susan Sorek, *The Jews Against Rome: War in Palestine AD 66-73* (London, 2008); Desmond Seward, *Jerusalem's Traitor: Josephus, Masada, and the Fall of Judea* (Cambridge, 2009); Shaye J.D. Cohen, *Josephus in Galilee and Rome* (Leiden, 1979); Seth Schwartz, *The Ruling Class of Judaea* (Cambridge, 1990).

For fact and myth at Masada: Yael Zerubavel, *Recovered Roots* (Chicago, 1995), chs. 5, 11; Raymond R. Newell, "The Forms and Historical Value of Josephus' Suicide Accounts," in Louis H. Feldman and Gohei Hata (eds.), *Josephus, The Bible and History* (Detroit, 1989); Nachman Ben-Yehuda, *The Masada Myth: Collective Memory and Mythmaking* (Madison, 1995).

For *sinat hinam* ("groundless hatred"), see the Talmudic text, Yoma 9b, accompanied by commentary in *The Talmud of the Land of Israel*, Vol. 14: Yoma, Tr. Jacob Neusner (Chicago, 1990). For analysis: Joel Gereboff, "Jewish Views of Hate: A Destructive But Permitted Emotion," in Joseph Telushkin, *A Code of Jewish Ethics, Vol. 1: You Shall Be Holy* (New York, 2006); Chana Safrai, "Morality and Stereotypes: Reflections on Yoma 9B," www.jewishfederations.org/page.aspx?id=77921.

Chapter 2. Conflict in Zion

The best analysis of the enduring conflict between left and right in Palestine/Israel is Ehud Sprinzak, *Brother Against Brother* (New York, 1999). Aspects of the Zionist Right are explored in Yaacov Shavit, *Jabotinsky and the Revisionist Movement 1925-1948* (London, 1988); Eran Kaplan, *The Jewish Radical Right: Revisionist Zionism and its Ideological Legacy* (Madison, 2005); Joseph Heller, *The Stern Gang* (London, 1995). For activities in the United States, see Rafael Medoff, *Militant Zionism in America* (Tuscaloosa, 2002).

The role of Chaim Arlosoroff in the transfer agreement of 1933 is carefully analyzed in Edwin Black, *The Transfer Agreement* (Washington, DC, 1999). For Arlosoroff's murder and the aftermath, see Nachman Ben-Yehuda, *Political Assassinations by Jews* (Albany, 1993).

The familiar story of the *Exodus* is expertly told in Aviva Halamish, *The Exodus Affair: Holocaust Survivors and the Struggle for Palestine*, Tr. Ora Cummings (Syracuse, 1998). See also Ruth Gruber, *Exodus 1947: The Ship That Launched a Nation* (New York, 1948), which popularized the episode; David C. Holly, *Exodus 1947* (Annapolis, 1969). For Bill Bernstein's experiences on board and his letters to his brother, see my "Lost Letters from the *Exodus*," *Forward* (September 4, 1992), 1. The role of the British Intelligence Agency is explored in Keith Jeffrey, *MI6: The History of the Secret Intelligence Service* (London, 2010).

Chapter 3. Civil War?

John Phillips, *A Will to Survive* (New York, 1976) is a vivid depiction, with interviews and photographs, of the fall of the Jewish Quarter in the Old City of Jerusalem. For the drafting of the Proclamation of Independence, Harold Fisch, *The Zionist Revolution* (New York, 1978), ch. 6, offers a superb analysis. See also David Ben-Gurion, *Israel: A Personal History* (New York, 1971), 76-78, 113; Asher Cohen and Bernard Susser, *Israel and the Politics of Jewish Identity: The Secular-Religious Impasse* (Baltimore, 2000); Dan Kurzman, *Genesis 1948* (New York, 1970).

My account of the *Altalena* journey and its consequences is constructed from many sources. The role of the Bergson Boys is explored in Judith Tydor Baumel, *The "Bergson Boys" and the Origins of Contemporary Zionist Militancy* (Syracuse, 2005). For the French role in supplying weapons and munitions, see Meir Zamir, "'Bid for Altalena': France's Covert Action in the 1948 War in Palestine," *Middle Eastern Studies* 46:1 (January 2010), 17-58; and for French-British conflict, his "Espionage and the Zionist Endeavor," *Jerusalem Post* (November 21, 2008). For Israeli government surveillance of the *Altalena* before its departure from France, see the testimony of Mayer Novik from the Israel Intelligence Service, File 201.00001, Haganah Archives.

The most comprehensive narrative of the journey appears in Eliahu Lankin, *To Win the Promised Land* (California, 1992). Also helpful is "The 'Altalena' Incident: Chronological Account," K 4-20-6, Jabotinsky Archives. For perceptive reflections by the youngest passenger: Saul Friedländer, *When Memory Comes*, Tr. Helen R. Lane (New York, 1979). Other passenger accounts include Mark Hasten, *Mark My Words* (United States, 2003); Nathan Cushman, Perry Foundeur, and Julian

BROTHERS AT WAR

Berenson, K 4-20-9, Jabotinsky Archives; Yitzhaq Ben-Ami, K 4-20-6, Jabotinsky Archives and *Years of Wrath, Days of Glory* (New York, 1982); Benyamin Telen, http://www.palyam.org/English/IS/Telem-Benyamin-Bini. Useful information appears in Alex Wilf, "The History of the Altalena," *The Answer* (July 9, 1948). The "Army Communique on Altalena Affair" appeared in *The Jewish Herald* (Johannesburg, July 2, 1948). General Staff instructions (June 22, 1948) are found in Shlomo Nakdimon, *Altalena* (Jerusalem, 1978), 162-63. Joe Kohn's descriptions are from his "Altalena Diary," *The Answer* (July 9, 1948). Arbal Zerubavel's testimony is in File 174.40, Haganah Archives. Israel Gorelnik's reminiscences are in File 32.3, Palmach Archives. For a sharp critique of Ben-Gurion during the *Altalena* crisis that includes many revealing details from participants, see Uri Milstein, *The Rabin File: An Unauthorized Exposé* (Jerusalem, 1999), 357-69.

My research assistant Sarah Trager located Moshe Lovy, "I Remember the 'Altalena,'" in the Yeshiva University Archives. Among other valuable documents, she also discovered the interview with Abba Groznick, transcribed by Nava Setter, and the poem by Rafael Khirs, translated from Hebrew by Sarah Honig in "A Memorial Candle," *Jerusalem Post* (September 21, 2007). See also Yoske Nachmias, "The Altalena Affair — Brother Against Brother" www.eretzisraelnet/welcome.asp. The recollection of Dr. Azriel Carlebach, editor of *Ma'ariv*, appeared in Nadi Matar, "Did Menachem Begin Err?" (July 4, 2004), www.antisemitism.no/articles/index. For the account of Uri Yarom: Sarah Honig, "The 'Altalena' Sequel," *Jerusalem Post* (July 16, 2007), citing his memoir, *Kenaf Renanim* (1971). See also "Begin's Arms Ship Ablaze on Seashore," *Palestine Post* (June 23, 1948); "Government Takes Firm Stand in Crisis," *Palestine Post* (June 23, 1948); "Cabinet Faces Crisis Over IZL," *Palestine Post* (June 24, 1948). For a report of "wide-scale arrests" of Irgun members after the attack: *Palestine Post* (June 25, 1948). By far the most vivid reporting appears in Arthur Koestler, "Trouble in Israel," *Manchester Guardian* (June 26, 1948). For the report of the American consulate to the Secretary of State (June 23, 1948), see K 4-20-29, Jabotinsky Archives.

BIBLIOGRAPHY

For a list of crew members, with additional information: "Enclosure to Confidential Dispatch No. 81, 1948," from S.W. Gray, Jabotinsky Archives, Tel Aviv, and "Altalena" http://israelvets.com/roster-aliyahbet-cres-ship.html#altalena. Captain Monroe Fein's revealing "Factual Account," written shortly after the attack on the *Altalena*, is in K 4-20-9, Jabotinsky Archives. See also Kohn, "Altalena Diary," *The Answer* (July 9, 1948); Jerry Salaman, Report (June 25, 1948), K 4-20-9, Jabotinsky Archives. For Boris Senior, who refused to attack the *Altalena*, see: "Obituary/A Founder of the Israel Air Force," haaretz.com (April 21, 2004). IDF soldiers killed during the two-day battle, whose names Avinoam Sharon located in the IDF Archives, were Moshe Chaim Katz and Zvi Reifer at Kfar Vitkin and Pesach Wolodinger at Palmach headquarters in Tel Aviv. For the names of the Irgun fighters who were killed, see the account of the memorialization of the *Altalena* in Chapter 5, pp. 123-24.

An extremely insightful film exploration, including many interviews with participants, is *Altalena*, Written and Directed by Ilana Tzur, Keshet Broadcasting Ltd. (1994). For its screening: Liat Collins, "'Altalena' Screened at Knesset," *Jerusalem Post* (January 4, 1995).

The following books were helpful for setting the *Altalena* episode in Israeli historical context: Peter Y. Medding, *The Founding of Israeli Democracy, 1948-1967* (New York, 1990); Anita Shapira, *Land and Power: The Zionist Resort to Force, 1881-1948* (Stanford, 1992); Eliot A. Cohen, *Supreme Command: Soldiers, Statesmen, and Leadership in Wartime* (New York, 2002). The best analysis of the *Altalena* episode within the history of political violence in Israel is Sprinzak, *Brother Against Brother*, ch. 1. Uri Dan's boyhood memory is recounted in "'Altalena' Rises Again," *Jerusalem Post* (August 28, 2003). A convenient summary can be found in Yehuda Lapidot, "The Altalena Affair," Jewish Virtual Library www.jewishvirtuallibrary.org.

BROTHERS AT WAR

Chapter 4. Competing Truths

For Menachem Begin: Menachem Begin, *The Revolt* (Tel Aviv, 1977) and "The Truth About the Altalena," Broadcast June 22, 1948, K 4-20-6, Jabotinsky Archives; Menachem Begin, "Secession, Saison, and the Altalena," *Ma'ariv* (August 13, 1971); Eitan Haber, *Menachem Begin: The Legend and the Man* (New York, 1979); Shmuel Katz, *Days of Fire* (London, 1968); Amos Perlmutter, *The Life and Times of Menachem Begin* (New York, 1987); J. Bowyer Bell, *Terror Out of Zion* (New York, 1977); Eric Silver, *Begin: The Haunted Prophet* (New York, 1984). For a highly partisan attempt to transform terrorism into a venerable Jewish tradition, see Ami Pedahzur and Arie Perliger, *Jewish Terrorism in Israel* (New York, 2009). Avi Shilon, *Begin: A Biography* (Hebrew) (Am Oved, 2007), notes how Begin's reputation has risen in Israel in recent years. He concludes that Begin "made an immense contribution to the crystallization of parliamentary democracy in Israel."

David Ben-Gurion's account of the *Altalena* appears in *Yoman Hamilchama: Milchemet Ha-atzma'ut, 1948-1949*, Gershon Rivlik and Elchanan Oren (eds.), Vol. 2 (Tel Aviv, 1984), 522, 526, 540-41, 543. The English title is *The War of Independence: Ben-Gurion's Diary*. See also Ben-Gurion, *Israel A Personal History* (Tel Aviv, 1971), 165-77. His Statement to the Provisional Council (June 23, 1948) is reprinted in Ben-Gurion, *Rebirth and Destiny of Israel*, Tr. by Mordekhai Nurock (New York, 1954). For Ben-Gurion's life before the proclamation of statehood, see Shabtai Teveth, *Ben-Gurion: The Burning Ground 1886-1948* (Boston, 1987). Michael Bar-Zohar, *Ben-Gurion: A Biography*, Tr. Peretz Kidron (London, 1978), had privileged access to Ben-Gurion's archives and personal papers. See also Robert St. John, *Ben-Gurion: The Biography of an Extraordinary Man* (New York, 1959), 159-63. For Yitzhak Rabin, see Dan Kurzman, *Soldier of Peace: The Life of Yitzhak Rabin* (New York, 1998), 134-39. Yitzhak Gruenbaum's warning can be found in Milstein, *History of the War of Independence*, Vol. I: 285. Rabin recalls the *Altalena* battle with Dov Goldstein in *Pinkas Sherut* (Tel Aviv, 1979), Vol. 2: 566-70. In the English translation (1979), the *Altalena* was not mentioned. His recollections also appear in an interview by Avraham Zohar (April 25, 1983) in the Beit HaPalmach Archives.

BIBLIOGRAPHY

For the Irgun perspective, in addition to the books and memoirs cited above: "Declaration by the Irgun Zvai Leumi" (June 23, 1948), K 4-20-6, Jabotinsky Archives; Shmuel Katz, "Report on Altalena, K 4-20-9, Jabotinsky Archives; Israel Eldad, *The First Tithe* (Jabotinsky Institute, 2008); Irgun Zvai Leumi B'Galut Britannia, "Truth About the Irgun Munition Ship" (Sivan 5708/June-July 1948), K 4-20-6, Jabotinsky Archives.

For an array of contemporary opinions: "Treason at Tel Aviv: Eye Witness Report on Irgun Ship Landing," by a Special Haganah Correspondent," Published by the National Committee for Labor Palestine, File 001/54481, Central Zionist Archives; "Ben Gurion Replies to Altalena Critics," *The Jewish Criterion* (August 13, 1948); Statement by Louis Bromfield (June 27, 1948); Hashomer Hatzair Youth Movement, n.d., F41/125, Central Zionist Archives (CZA), Jerusalem; "These Are the Facts," Irgun Radio Broadcast (June 26, 1948) in *The Answer* (July 9, 1948); Henry Morgenthau, Jr., telegram (June 23, 1948), A364/823, CZA; George Barrett, "Israel-Irgun Fight a Sham, Arab Says," *The New York Times* (July 14, 1948); Arthur Koestler, "Tel Aviv Fighting: Government's Motives in Stopping Irgun," *Manchester Guardian* (June 24, 1948) and "Trouble in Israel," *Manchester Guardian* (June 26, 1948); "House Divided," *Time* (July 5, 1948), 28-29; Report Dated 16 September 1948 by the United Nations Mediator on the Observation of the Truce in Palestine During the Period From 11 June to 9 July 1948; Merrill Simon, *Moshe Arens: Statesman and Scientist Speaks Out* (New York, 1988), 117.

The first complete accounts of the *Altalena* were Shlomo Nakdimon, *Altalena* (Jerusalem, 1978) and Uri Brenner, *Altalena: A Political History and Military Study* (Tel Aviv, 1978), both in Hebrew. See also Arthur Koestler's *Palestine Diary 1948*, Koestler Archives, University of Edinburgh, ynetnews.com (September 4, 2005); Asa Aron, "Avar Bemhaloket — Yitzug Mefutzal" ("Past in Contention-Divergent Presentation"), Master of Arts Paper (n.d.), Hebrew University, Jerusalem, offers an insightful analysis of the competing narratives.

Other helpful secondary sources, in addition to those cited above, include: Shlomo Avineri, *The Making of Modern Zionism* (New York, 1981); Larry Collins and Dominique Lapierre, *O, Jerusalem* (New York, 1972); Tom Segev, *1949: The First Israelis* (New York, 1986); Dan Kurzman, *Ben-Gurion: Prophet of Fire* (New York, 1983); Sasson Sofer, *Begin: An Anatomy of Leadership* (Oxford, 1988); Joseph Heller, *The Birth of Israel, 1945-1949: Ben-Gurion and his Critics* (Gainesville, FL, 2000); Yigal Allon, *The Making of Israel's Army* (New York, 1970); Anita Shapira, *Yigal Allon, Native Son* (Philadelphia, 2008); Leslie Stein, *The Making of Modern Israel 1948-1967* (Cambridge, 2009); Colin Shindler, *The Land Beyond Promise* (London, 2002); Michael Keren, "Biography and Historiography: The Case of David Ben-Gurion," *Biography*, 23:2 (Spring 2000), 332-51.

For Israeli government efforts to erase the *Altalena* from history, see Udi Lebel, "'Beyond the Pantheon': Bereavement, Memory, and the Strategy of De-Legitimization Against Herut," *Israel Studies*, 10:3 (Fall 2005), 104-26.

Chapter 5. Memories

Begin's Knesset comments appear in *Divrei HaKnesset* (Knesset Proceedings), 3 Shevat 5712 (12 January 1959), 826, 828. "Irgun Ship Sinking Marked by Israelis," *The New York Times* (June 13, 1949); William Safire, "The Altalena Docks," *The New York Times* (July 14, 1977); Anthony Lewis, "A Fateful Choice," *The New York Times* (April 17, 1988); Samuel Schachter letter to *The New York Times* (October 20, 1994).

For renewed attention to Yitzhak Rabin's role in the *Altalena* after the Oslo Accords: Yoram Peri, "The Assassination: Causes, Meaning, Outcomes" in Peri (ed.), *The Assassination of Yitzhak Rabin* (Stanford, 2000), 304, 370. The call for a Palestinian *Altalena* is explored in Moshe Arens, "Peres and Arafat's Altalena," www.haaretz.com (October 16, 2001); Uri Avnery, "The Sacred Cannon," *CounterPunch* (June 3, 2003); Moshe Maoz, "Waiting for Abu Mazen's Altalena," www.forward.com (July 18, 2003); *Arutz-7* (September 1, 2003); Ido Aviani, "Altalena

BIBLIOGRAPHY

Shelanu Ve-Shelahem" ("Our Altalena and Theirs"), *De'ot* (April 3, 2005); Gad Nahshon, "'Altalena Affair' A Blood Libel — June 22, 1948," *JewishPost*, www.jewishpost.com/archives/news/altalena-affair-a-blood-libel-1.html.

For settlers, religious Zionism and the *Altalena*: Uri Dan, "'Altalena' Rises Again," *Jerusalem Post* (August 27, 2003); Arik Bender, "Haim Hefer v. Ruby Rivlin," *Ma'ariv* (November 25, 2004); Yaron London, "Altalena vs. Disengagement," *Israel Opinion* (June 29, 2005); Shmuel Katz, "Don't Invoke the 'Altalena,'" *Jerusalem Post* (July 27, 2005); Nadav Shragai, "The Opposition/Refusal Groups Hope Altalena Anniversary will Boost Support," www.haaretz.com (June 23, 2005); Yosef Salmon, "What Happened to Religious Zionism?," www.haaretz.com (August 15, 2005); Myles Kantor, "A Culture of Repression," *Arutz-7* (April 12, 2007); Yoav Zitun, "Protestors: Har Bracha Students Pressured to Leave Yeshiva," ynet.news.com (March 24, 2010); Hillel Fendel, "Banner Wavers Returned to Hesder," *Arutz-7* (July 12, 2010); Chaim Levenson, "Yeshiva Students to Court: Give IDF Status Back to Har Bracha," www.haaretz.com (January 1, 2010); Shlomo Avineri, "On Zionism and Refusing Orders," www.haaretz.com (December 21, 2009); Yehuda Ben Meir, "A Courageous Decision," www.haaretz.com (December 20, 2009); Gershom Gorenberg, *Accidental Empire: Israel and the Birth of Settlements, 1967-1977* (New York, 2006), 4-5, 273-74, 282-86, 336.

For Yesh Gvul and other protests by soldiers: http.yeshgvul.org/about_e.asp; and http://seruv.org.il/english/article.asp?msgid=55&type=news (September 25, 2003). Rabbinic disagreement over settlement expulsion and disobedience is explored in Gadi Taub, *The Settlers And the Struggle over the Meaning of Zionism* (New Haven, 2010), 144-47.

For Russian immigrants: Lili Galili, "New Immigrants Shape Their Identity Around the Altalena Story," www.haaretz.com (July 20, 2007).

BROTHERS AT WAR

Epilogue

For Ben-Gurion's admiration for American history: Kurzman, *Ben-Gurion: Prophet of Fire*, 114. The Whiskey Rebellion is recounted in Gordon S. Wood, *Empire of Liberty: A History of the Early Republic, 1789—1815* (New York, 2009), 134-38. Suggested parallels (and differences) are mine. Efraim Karsh, *Palestine Betrayed* (New Haven, 2010), documents the considerable responsibility of Palestinians for their own plight as refugees.

Acknowledgments

During a conversation with my dear Israeli friend Haggai about Israel's nagging problem of legitimacy, I mentioned the *Altalena*. Instantly his expression changed. (He had fought as a Palmach soldier in the War of Independence.) He reminded me of the 1st century Zealots in Jerusalem, whose war against their fellow Jews — so Josephus had recorded — was responsible for the collapse of Jewish national sovereignty and the subsequent rabbinical warning against *sinat hinam*. Haggai's instant identification of the *Altalena* with the Zealots of Jewish antiquity planted the seed that germinated in this book. But he is in no way responsible for its content or conclusions. In our enduring friendship of thirty-five years, we have always remained brothers at peace.

Brothers at War exists as both an electronic and a "real" book due to the initiative, expertise and guidance of Alan Childress, publisher of Quid Pro Books. His attentiveness to my own wishes as an author is deeply appreciated. With Peretz Rodman as our matchmaker, Avinoam Sharon became my Hebrew translator — and, unexpectedly, my valued instructor in many facets of Israeli military culture. Miriam Sharon located important bibliographical information. Sarah Trager (Wellesley College '13) was a resourceful and imaginative research assistant, whose discoveries — including the cover photograph — are sprinkled throughout this book. Students in my Wellesley seminars on the history of Israel asked good questions and offered thoughtful answers.

Archivists in Israel at the Menachem Begin Heritage Center, the Central Zionist Archives, the Jabotinsky Institute Archives, the Etzel Museum, the Beit HaPalmach Archives, the Haganah Archives and the David Ben-Gurion Archives facilitated my research. Yisrael Medad and Ori Rub at the Begin Center, Amira Stern at the Jabotinsky Institute, and Eldad Harouvi at the Palmach Archives were especially helpful. *Jerusalem Post* columnist Sarah Honig gave permission to publish her translation of the Rafael Khirs poem, which first appeared in her article, "A Memorial Candle." The National Photo Collection of the Government Press Office in Israel, the Jabotinsky Institute, the United States Holocaust Museum, and Magnum Photos permitted me to reprint photographs. Once again, Wellesley College generously funded my research and travel.

As the beneficiary of corrections, comments, and suggestions from perceptive readers of various drafts of my manuscript, I am exceedingly grateful to my son Jeff and to Dan Horowitz, Steve Whitfield, Neil Hecht, Bill Novak, and Yisrael Medad for their valuable contributions. They are entirely blameless for any remaining errors, whether of fact or interpretation, for which I alone am responsible.

Members of my family respected my need for solitude to think and write and tolerated my more exasperating eccentricities. Shira guided me through the legal labyrinth of contract and copyright issues and Susan untangled my (usually self-inflicted) computer glitches. Pasha was my constantly delightful companion. I am blessed with my children, Jeffrey, Pamela, Shira, and Rebecca, and my grandchildren, Cole, Dalia and Jonah. No less precious, yet again, was Susan's patient and sustaining love.

JSA

January 2011

About the Author

Jerold S. Auerbach has been identified as "America's foremost intellectual exponent of right-wing Zionism." His books include *Unequal Justice: Lawyers and Social Change in Modern America* (1976), a *New York Times* Noteworthy Book; *Justice Without Law?* (1983); *Rabbis and Lawyers: The Journey From Torah to Constitution* (1990, 2010); *Jacob's Voices: Reflections of a Wandering American Jew* (1996, 2010); *Are We One? Jewish Identity in the United States and Israel* (2001); *Explorers in Eden: Pueblo Indians and the Promised Land* (2006); and *Hebron Jews: Memory and Conflict in the Land of Israel* (2009). His extensive writings have appeared in the *Wall Street Journal, Commentary, Midstream, The Jewish Press, The New York Times, Jerusalem Post, Outpost,* and online publications.

Auerbach has been a Guggenheim Fellow, Fulbright Lecturer at Tel Aviv University, Visiting Scholar at the Harvard Law School, and the recipient of two College Teachers Fellowships from the National Endowment for the Humanities.

He is Professor Emeritus of History at Wellesley College, where he taught for forty years.

Index

ahavat hinam, 142
Ahimeir, Abba, 22-23
Allon, Yigal, 67, 69, 100
Altalena
    arrival in Israel, 59-60, 92, 103
    as reflecting later unresolved internal issues, 109, 115, 122, 125-126, 133-134, 135-136, 142
    contemporary analogies to and uses of, 125-134, 135-136, 142
    departure from France, 53-54
    later accounts by participants, 91-102, 104-108
    linkage with Jerusalem, 74
    memorial ceremonies, 117, 118, 124, 130
    monument to, 123-124
    munitions aboard, 52, 63
    notification of ceasefire, 54-56
    origins of ship and name, 43
    portrayal in film, 100, 122
    response among American Jews, 102
    response in the Knesset, 108-109
    response in United Nations, 103
    siege and destruction of, 63-72, 78, 87-88, 117
    sinking of wreckage, 117
    violation of ceasefire, 56, 62, 103, 110
Altneuland, 3

American Zion, 2
appeasement, 25
Arafat, Yasir, 123, 124-125
Arens, Moshe, 108, 124
Ariel, Shmuel, 48
Arlosoroff, Chaim, 20-24, 26, 38, 39, 43, 58, 68, 90, 102, 108, 118, 139
Avineri, Shlomo, 132
Balfour Declaration, 19
Barak, Ehud, 132-133
Bar-Zohar, Michael, 30, 89, 99, 110
Begin, Menachem
    and arrival of *Altalena*, 60
    and Herut party, 77, 109, 117
    and Independence, 38, 46-47
    and Irgun, 20, 24, 27-30, 33, 42, 47, 57-58, 60, 63, 69, 71, 76-77, 86, 90-93, 101, 104-106, 111-112-113, 117, 139
    and notification of ceasefire, 54-57
    anticipating negotiations, 56, 62-64, 105, 140
    as Prime Minister, 100, 109, 112, 133
    dissolution of Irgun, 77
    later accounts of *Altalena* incident, 91-94, 104-105, 108-109
    leaving destroyed *Altalena*, 72
    overview, 3, 5-6, 89-92

perception among biographers, 111-115
perception in United States, 102
reconciliation surrounding Six-Day War, 120-121
reparations, German, dispute over, 118-120

Ben-Ami, Yitzhaq, 41, 42, 52, 63, 107-108

Ben-Eliezer, Arieh, 41

Ben-Gurion, David
analogies to George Washington, 136-139
and *Altalena* munitions and arrival, 50, 53, 57, 61, 76, 92, 98, 103, 105-106, 111
and Independence, 36-39, 44, 46-47, 50, 81, 136
and Irgun, 20, 26-28, 30, 32, 35, 58-59, 62, 66, 69, 72, 74-75, 90-97, 107, 113-114, 125
biographies of, laudatory, 110-111, 113, 114
characterization of his actions against *Altalena*, 75, 89, 94-98
consolidation of power, 99-101, 104, 107-108, 109-110, 112, 114-115, 117, 120, 133, 135, 139-140
criticism from cabinet, 74-75
endorsing a commission of inquiry, 109
memorial service for, 124

orders re *Altalena*, 61-62, 65-67, 69-70, 92
overview 3, 5-6, 89-91, 94
reconciliation surrounding Six-Day War, 120-121
reparations, from Germany, dispute over, 118-120

ben Yair, Elazar, 11-12

ben Zakkai, Yohanan, 13-14, 38, 43

Bergson Boys, 41-42, 107

Brenner, Uri, 110

British Mandatory Rule, 19-21, 24-25, 34, 44, 90-91, 95, 104, 140, 142

Brother Against Brother (Sprinzak), 114

Cahan, Yaakov, 15

Cain and Abel, 3, 90, 118, 120, 130

Churchill, Winston, 19, 29, 35

civil war, 1, 3, 5, 7, 9, 17, 27, 29, 39, 41, 66-67, 74, 90, 94-97, 102, 104-105, 107, 111-115, 122, 124, 127, 129, 136, 138, 142. *See also* putsch.

Dayan, Moshe, 61

Dulles, John Foster, 118

Entebbe, raid on airport in Uganda, 141

Etzel Museum, 118

Exodus, 3, 4, 31-35, 43, 53, 60, 139, 141

Fein, Monroe, 43, 47, 50, 53, 55, 60, 65, 70, 72-73, 83

INDEX

France, provision of munitions, 49-50

Friedländer, Pavel, 51-52, 55

Friedman, Thomas, 125

Galili, Yisrael, 46-47, 52, 56-58, 61-62, 66-67, 69, 76, 98, 105-106

Germany, offer of reparations, 118-120. *See also* Holocaust; Nazis and Nazism.

Golomb, Eliahu, 27-28

Goodman, Martin, 9-10

Gorenberg, Gershom, 126-127

Green, Aaron, 51

Gruner, Dov, 33

Guardian, The, 111

Haaretz, 124, 127-128, 130, 132

Haber, Eitan, 29

Haganah, 27, 29-30, 44-46, 67, 70, 73, 89, 93, 95, 100, 103, 106, 117, 122-123, 127, 135

halacha, 131

Halamish, Aviva, 31

havlaga, 24

Hazit Haam, 22

Hebron, massacre in, 20

Heller, Joseph, 112

Herut party, 77, 109, 117, 118, 128, 139

Hitler, Adolf, 1, 21, 93, 119

Holocaust, 15, 51, 62-63, 118, 139

"holy cannon," 97, 117, 129, 140

immigration, 1-3

Irgun (IZL), 3-4, 24-25, 28-29, 30, 33, 35, 42, 46-48, 50, 52, 54-55, 61-69, 75-77, 86, 90, 95-97, 100-103, 106-108, 110, 112-114, 117-118, 122-125, 139

Isaac and Ishmael, 3, 141

Israel, State of
    declaration of independence, in 1948, 1, 17, 36, 81, 112, 136
    fear expressed of internal rebellion, 3, 5, 59, 65-67, 69, 89, 95-98, 100-101, 107, 109-114, 123, 127, 139
    identity struggle over state's definition, 135
    settlements and settlers, 125-130, 133, 135
    Six-Day War, 17, 120, 140-141
    See also Jerusalem; Mandate, British; Tel Aviv.

IZL. *See* Irgun.

Jabotinsky, Eri, 41, 68, 77

Jabotinsky, Vladimir (Ze'ev), 20, 23, 41, 43, 91, 101, 103

Jerusalem
    1st century, destruction and civil war, 1, 19, 77
    control and jurisdiction over, 74-75
    linkage between city and *Altalena*, 74
    partitioned in 1947, 44-46
    protest over German reparations, 119
    See also King David Hotel; Israel, State of.

Jerusalem Post, 125
Josephus, Flavius, 7-14, 17, 63, 90
Jotapata, siege of, 7-8
Katz, Shmuel, 101, 128-129
Kfar Vitkin, 64, 73, 92, 96, 104, 114, 138, 140
Khirs, Rafael, 77-78, 117
kibbutz, 21, 29, 9
King David Hotel, 30, 44, 90
Koestler, Arthur, 103-104
Kohn, Joe, 51, 68
Kook, Abraham Yitzhak haCohen, 41, 142
Kook, Hillel, 35, 41-42, 73, 77
Kurzman, Dan, 110-111
Lankin, Eliahu, 27, 43, 48-49, 52, 54-58, 60-62, 64, 68, 71-73, 77, 84, 90, 101, 105-106
Lamdan, Yitzhak, 15
Lebel, Udi, 117
Lehi, 29-30, 46-47, 76-77, 94-95, 112, 118
Lewis, Anthony, 121-122
Ma'ariv, 71, 76, 105
Manchester Guardian, 103
Mandate, British, over Palestine, 19-21, 24-25, 34, 44, 90-91, 104, 140, 142
Maoz, Moshe, 125
Maron, Asa, 117
Masada, 11-12, 15-17
McLaren, James, 10

Medding, Peter, 113
military orders, refusal to follow, 131-134
Milstein, Uri, 113-114
munitions
  aboard *Altalena*, listing of, 52, 63
  notification to Ben-Gurion, 50, 53
  provision by France, 49-50
Nakdimon, Shlomo, 109-110
Nazis and Nazism
  analogies to, 101-102, 119
  generally, 1, 15, 21-22, 23-24, 26, 118
  See also Holocaust; Hitler, Adolf; Germany.
Neusner, Jacob, 14
New York Times, 110, 121-122, 125
Noah's ark, 1
Palmach, 15, 27, 29, 44, 46-47, 58, 60, 67-69, 71, 89, 91, 95, 98-100, 110, 112, 117, 122-123, 128, 130, 135
Patria, 2
Port-du-Bouc, 34, 42, 50, 52, 54, 56, 101, 105
Proskauer, Joseph M., 41
putsch, asserted anticipation of, 3, 5, 59, 65-67, 69, 89, 95-98, 100-101, 107, 109-114, 120, 123, 127, 139
Rabin, Yitzhak, 67-68, 70, 72, 91, 98, 100, 113, 115, 123, 126, 130-131
Reparations, to be paid by Germany, dispute over, 118-120
Revolt, The, 93-94, 104

INDEX

Roosevelt, Franklin D., 42

St. Louis, 2

Saison, 28. *See also* Season.

Safire, William, 121

Samuels, Gertrude, 110

Shilansky, Dov, 62-63, 122

Season, The, 28-30, 67, 90-91, 94, 101, 107, 114

Sharon, Ariel, 124, 125-126, 129

Shaltiel, David, 44, 46

Shapira, Anita, 99, 108, 113

Silver, Eric, 111

sicarii, 9, 11, 22, 38

sinat hinam, 4, 13-14, 115, 142

Six-Day War (1967), 17, 120, 140-141

Sneh, Moshe, 30

Sofer, Sasson, 112

Sprinzak, Ehud, 23, 114-115

Stavsky, Avraham, 23, 42-43, 52, 55-56, 64, 68, 72, 124, 139

Stolier, David, 2

Struma, 2

Tel Aviv, 64, 73, 92, 96, 104, 118, 138, 140, 141

Teveth, Shabtai, 99

Time, 102

transfer agreement, 118

Tzur, Ilana, 122

Wars of the Jews, 7-9, 11

Washington, George, 136-139

Washington Post, 110

weapons. *See* munitions.

Weber, Max, 6

Weizmann, Chaim, 28, 29

Whiskey Rebellion, in U.S. history, 136-138

Wise, Stephen S., 41

World Zionist Organization, 28

Yom Kippur War, 17

Yadin, Yigael, 15-16, 47, 61, 65, 73, 98

Zamir, Meir, 49

Zerubavel, Arbel, 69

Zerubavel, Yael, 15-16, 17

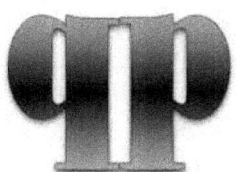

Visit us at www.quidprobooks.com

www.ingramcontent.com/pod-product-compliance
Lightning Source LLC
Chambersburg PA
CBHW071848230426
43671CB00012B/2100